WHATEVER HAPPENED

TO THE

WRATH

OF GOD?

JOHN MUNCY

ETHNOS Press
Pittsburgh, Pennsylvania

Dedication

To my closest and dearest friend, Carolyn. Only God could bless me with such a wonderful wife. Thank you for standing with me and being my greatest source of encouragement and strength on this earth. I appreciate you more than words can say.

To my firstborn, Bethany Grace. You are a precious young lady with such a sweet spirit. I will never cease to praise God for extending our time together. You are truly the best daughter a dad could ever dream of. I love you so much.

To the greatest boy God ever made, Titus Matthew. Your character, love for God and stand for righteousness are awesome! I look forward to many more years of fun with you. I love you and am so proud to call you my son.

And finally to my endless source of joy, Moriah Faith. Even though you are much too young to read this, I want to tell you how thankful I am for such a big blessing in such a small package! It excites me to think of the joy you will bring to the Kingdom of God as you continue to grow. I love you, sweetheart!

Acknowledgments

It's with a grateful heart that I would like to acknowledge the following people for making this book a reality:

Pastor Tim Tracy and the precious brothers and sisters at Family Christian Center. Tim, your encouragement and openness to our ministry has always been so uplifting. Thank you for believing in me and my message and for opening your pulpit to my preaching. Thank you for the many check-up phone calls and for paving the way for this book.

Jack and Debbie Broughton. When I look up "friends" in my dictionary, your pictures are there! You both are such a breath of fresh air. Miles have not separated our hearts. Thanks for all the meals, laughs, tears, support, advice and everything else you both have added to our lives. Thank you for believing in us and helping us get this book in print. Your rewards are waiting!

Joe and Arlene Plake, and your three precious children, Mandy, April and Justin. In the short time we've known each other, it's amazing how our hearts have been united. Thank you so much for making this book become a reality! God bless you!

Tom and Stephanie Moore. An awesome couple whose devotion to Jesus and His work is equally awesome. Thank you both for your faithful support of our ministry down through the years!

Neil and Trudy Erisman and your three wonderful children. You all are such an encouragement. What a testimony you have become. Thank you for your willingness and faithfulness in supporting our ministry.

David and Ann Drye and your precious family. David, I see you as one of the greatest men of God I know! Thank you for your uncompromising stand for God and His Word. Thank you for all you've done for me and my family. You've made a major impact on my life!!

Pastor David Kirkwood. A man who has proved his love for God's Word in all his preaching, teaching and writings. Your stand for sound doctrine speaks volumes to a world of Christians with itching ears. May our Lord continue to use you and Ethnos Press to publish the unadulterated truth of the Word, for truly "the whole world needs to know."

Toni and Jane Ivanhoe. Your eagle-eye editing has saved me much embarassment!

Gail Hoppe. Thanks for using your skills on the layout and design of the text and cover. People do judge a book by its cover, and you've designed an awesome one.

To the many generous friends of this ministry! Thank you for helping us fulfill God's call on our lives. God alone is able to repay you all!

Table of Contents

Introduction

*For the time will come when they will not endure sound
doctrine; but after their own lusts shall they heap to
themselves teachers, having itching ears;
And they shall turn away their ears from the truth, and
shall be turned unto fables (2 Tim. 4:3-4).*

*Study to show thyself approved unto God,
a workman that needeth not to be ashamed,
rightly dividing the word of truth (2 Tim. 2:15).*

The book you are about to read requires two things: a Bible
and an honest heart. Sad to say, too many Christians
have become comfortable with having neither. If they don't
agree with something they've read in the Scriptures, they
simply ignore it or find a book or teaching tape that explains
it away. Human opinions have replaced the Bible as the final
authority for truth.

I suggest you keep an open Bible nearby as you read.

You'll find hundreds of scripture verses cited or quoted. Don't skip over them. Read them carefully. Become like the Bereans whom the Bible says "were more noble than those in Thessalonica, in that they received the word with all readiness of mind, and searched the scriptures daily, whether those things were so" (Acts 17:11).

Perhaps you've heard, as I have, preaching or teaching that contradicted the Scriptures. Many years ago, when I began reading the Word of God, just as a young boy, I noticed there were hundreds of examples of God doing things that some people said He never does. I remember hearing sermons and reading books that claimed God was in no way responsible for calamities, bad weather, destructive storms, accidents, deaths or anything negative. These were all attributed to the devil's doing. They made it seem as if Satan was controlling more than God was. Some even promoted the idea that God's hands are tied from operating on the earth and that humanity must somehow win back the world by taking authority over Satan. Sad to say, many have swallowed the concepts of an all-powerful devil, an exalted man and an undersized God. So many have been guilty of twisting Scripture to their "own destruction" (2 Peter 3:16).

But, as you read the pages that follow and note the many scriptures I've cited, you'll see an entirely different picture of what God is like. You'll learn that He is sovereign, reigning with supreme control. He is the only Potentate, the exalted King who has the final say in all things. This awesome Lord demands our fear and reverence.

The second thing you will need is an honest heart. Is your heart honest with the Word of God? Every Christian should accept nothing but the truth concerning God's character as it is revealed in the Bible. In the parable of the sower and the seed, we read that it is the person with an honest heart who allows the Word to become fruitful in his life:

> But that on the good ground are they, which in an *honest and good heart*, having heard the word, keep it, and bring forth fruit with patience" (Luke 8:15; emphasis added).

How can we honestly teach that there is a heaven but neglect to teach that there is a hell? How can we say that God is a God of love but not mention that He is also a God of wrath? How can we ignore the apostle Paul's reference to the "goodness and *severity* of God" (Rom. 11:22, emphasis added)?

I challenge you to *always* be honest with the Word of God as you read it. Whatever it says, believe it! Act on it! How often have you heard someone say, "God said it; I believe it, and that settles it"? But the truth is, if God said it, that settles it! Whether we believe it or not, it's still true.

Chances are, you've already thought somewhat about the subject of the wrath of God or you wouldn't have picked up this book. There's no doubt that it's a controversial subject in many Christian circles. Nothing seems harder for the modern church to swallow than the fact that "the Lord is a God of judgment" (Isaiah 30:18). We've conveniently by-passed such verses, ignoring their importance and denying the truth.

In his classic book, *Knowing God*, J. I. Packer writes about God's wrath,

> The modern habit throughout the Christian church is to play this subject down. Those who still believe in the wrath of God (not all do) say little about it; perhaps they

do not think much about it. To an age which has unashamedly sold itself to the gods of greed, pride, sex and self-will, the church mumbles on about God's kindness but says virtually nothing about His judgment. How often during the past year did you hear, or, if you are a minister, did you preach, a sermon on the wrath of God? How long is it, I wonder, since a Christian spoke straight on this subject on radio or television, or in one of those half-column sermonettes that appear in some national dailies and magazines? (And if one did so, how long would it be before he would be asked to speak or write again?) The fact is that the subject of divine wrath has become taboo in modern society, and Christians by and large have accepted the taboo and conditioned themselves never to raise the matter.[1]

My prayer is that your heart will be honest as you read what follows, allowing God's Word to cause you to tremble (see Isaiah 66:1-2,5).

John Muncy

[1]*Knowing God*, J. I. Packer, pp. 148-149

ONE

The Wrath of God is Revealed

*For the wrath of God is revealed from heaven against all
ungodliness and unrighteousness of men, who hold the
truth in unrighteousness* (Rom. 1:18).

When was the last time you heard a message or read a
book on the wrath of God? I can hardly remember
hearing or reading anything about God's wrath during my
entire Christian life (except for what I've read in the Bible).

Visit your local Christian bookstore and ask for a book on
the subject of God's wrath. I have. I was told there wasn't
much available on the subject due to the fact that, as one
bookstore manager explained, "God's wrath is not a very
popular subject." Popular or not, God's wrath is a biblical
truth. It seems that, although the wrath of God has been
"revealed from heaven," it has become "concealed on earth"!

The message of God's wrath is so evident in the Bible that
a person would have to be dishonest to deny it. As David

Kirkwood states in his book, *God's Tests*:

> God is merciful, but He is also a judge. If we had the
> space, we could look at hundreds of examples in the
> Bible of God's judgment upon people and nations. In
> addition, we could look at hundreds of warnings of
> God's judgment upon people, nations and the entire
> world. Of the sixty-six books in the Bible, I can only
> find five (all very short books) that don't mention or in
> some way intimate the judgment of God.[1]

Is not true justice characterized by a just and righteous
reaction against sin? If we expect a human judge to act with
righteousness toward a transgressor, how much more should
we expect the same of God, whose righteousness is perfect?

Jesus, who is God incarnate and therefore the personifica-
tion of truth and love, spoke more about judgment, wrath and
hell than anyone else in the New Testament. In fact, He spoke
more about those subjects than all the other New Testament
writers *combined*. Then why do so many of His followers
disregard this important truth? Do they think they can de-
claw and de-fang the Lion of the tribe of Judah?

Noted author, Arthur W. Pink, wrote,

> A study of the concordance will show that there are
> more references in Scripture to the anger, fury, and
> wrath of God, than there are to His love and tenderness.
> Because God is holy, He hates all sin; and because He
> hates all sin, His anger burns against the sinner.[2]

Why are we so prone to avoid this subject? Perhaps it's
because we'd rather not think of God as He has revealed
Himself in His Word. Yet He certainly has not hidden His

---

[1]*God's Tests*, David S. Kirkwood, pp. 127-128
[2]*The Attributes of God*, Arthur W. Pink, pp. 82-83

true character from us. The wrath of God is revealed very thoroughly in the Bible, so it's obvious that God desires that we know of His wrath, anger, indignation and fury. It's only in understanding this aspect of His character that we can comprehend how serious God is about sin. Pastor John MacArthur writes,

> How could One who delights only in what is pure and lovely not loathe what is impure and ugly? How could He who is infinitely holy disregard sin, which by its very nature violates that holiness? How could He who loves righteousness not hate and act severely against all unrighteousness? How could He who is the sum of all excellency look with complacency on virtue and vice equally? He cannot do those things, because He is holy, just, and good. Wrath is the only just response a perfectly holy God could make to unholy men. Righteous wrath therefore is every bit as much an element of God's divine perfection as any other of His attributes.[3]

If we fail to comprehend the intensity of God's hatred of sin, we will never understand the immensity of His mercy. Unless we can grasp something about His wrath, we will never begin to fathom His grace. Truly, it is God's furious indignation against sin that makes the good news so good. No one seeks a cure for a disease he doesn't possess. In the same way, sinners have no reason to seek salvation until they realize the dire consequences of their rebellion. It's no wonder Satan fights so hard to keep this truth neglected.

The biblical method of presenting the gospel has always been warning sinners of the wrath to come and then revealing the way of escape. Before God's pardon can make any sense, His judgment upon sin must be understood. Eternal life is for

---

[3]*Romans*, John MacArthur, Jr., pp. 74

those who are facing eternal death. The entire message of the loving, redeeming grace of God being offered through Christ rests upon the fact that humanity has rejected God and is thus under the sentence of His eternal wrath. Again, Arthur W. Pink writes,

> The wrath of God is a perfection of the Divine character upon which we need to frequently meditate. First, that our hearts may be duly impressed by God's detestation of sin. We are ever prone to regard sin lightly, to gloss over its hideousness, to make excuses for it. But the more we study and ponder God's abhorrence of sin and His frightful vengeance upon it, the more likely are we to realize its heinousness. Secondly, to beget a true fear in our souls for God: "Let us have grace whereby we may serve God acceptably with reverence and godly fear: for our God is a consuming fire" (Heb. 12:28,29). We cannot serve Him "acceptably" unless there is due righteous anger; and these are best promoted by frequently calling to mind that "our God is a consuming fire." Thirdly, to draw out our souls in fervent praise for our having been delivered from "the wrath to come" (1 Thes. 1:10).[4]

Yet still another reason to consider this doctrine so vital is because of its power to motivate us to evangelism. Knowing of God's wrath should cause us to be zealous to preach Christ with passion and urgency. The church's soul-winning drive languishes when God's wrath is disregarded.

The great Bible teacher and soul winner, R. A. Torrey, wisely wrote,

> Shallow views of sin and of God's holiness, and of the glory of Jesus Christ and His claims upon us, lie at the

---

[4]*The Attributes of God*, Arthur W. Pink, pp. 84-85

16

bottom of weak theories of the doom of the impenitent. When we see sin in all its hideousness and enormity, the Holiness of God in all its perfection, and the glory of Jesus Christ in all its infinity, nothing but a doctrine that those who persist in the choice of sin, who love darkness rather than light, and who persist in the rejection of the Son of God, shall endure everlasting anguish, will satisfy the demands of our own moral intuitions....The more closely men walk with God and the more devoted they become to His service, the more likely they are to believe this doctrine....If you in any wise abate the doctrine, it will abate your zeal. Time and again the author has come up to this awful doctrine and tried to find some way of escape from it, but when he has failed, as he always has at last, when he was honest with the Bible and with himself, he has returned to his work with an increased burden for souls and an intensified determination to spend and be spent for their salvation.[5]

[5]*What the Bible Teaches*, R. A. Torrey, pp. 311-313

TWO

A Message to the Friends of God

Then said he [John] to the multitude that came forth to be baptized of him, "O generation of vipers, who hath warned you to flee from the wrath to come?" (Luke 3:7)

Knowing therefore the terror of the Lord, we persuade men... (2 Cor. 5:11)

L et's begin by reading the following words of Jesus found in Luke 12:4-5. Please read them very carefully.

"And I say unto you my friends, Be not afraid of them that kill the body, and after that have no more that they can do. But I will forewarn you whom ye shall fear: Fear him, which after he hath killed hath power to cast into hell; yea, I say unto you, Fear him."

Some would take such a statement to be a threat spoken to enemies. Yet Jesus said those words to His disciples, calling them His "friends." He was simply sharing a statement of fact: God can kill you and can cast you into hell, so you had better fear Him.

We do a great disservice by not telling people the truth about fearing God. We're afraid we might offend them. The truth is that we have more fear of men than we do of God. But the one who truly fears God will not fear man!

Jesus told us whom not to fear: "Be not afraid of them that kill the body, and after that have no more that they can do." No doubt some of the very people who heard Jesus say those words became martyrs. Yet after they died nothing more could be done to them. Their death was their entrance into glory! But in the same breath, Jesus said there is One of whom we must be afraid: "Fear him, which after he hath killed hath power to cast into hell; yea, I say unto you, Fear him."

The church has been guilty of teaching a watered-down fear of God. It has been based on human standards. This Isaiah spoke of:

> Wherefore the Lord said, "Forasmuch as this people draw near me with their mouth, and with their lips do honour me, but have removed their heart far from me, and their fear toward me is taught by the precept [standards] of men" (Isaiah 29:13).

Today, most believe that fearing God is little more than reverencing or respecting Him. Certainly we should reverence God, but that alone is not fearing Him. Consider the following verse that so clearly shows reverence and godly fear as two separate things:

> Wherefore we are receiving a kingdom which cannot be moved, let us have grace, whereby we may serve

God acceptably with *reverence and godly fear*: For our God is a consuming fire (Hebrews 12:28-29, emphasis added).

If godly fear simply means "reverence," why doesn't this verse read, "reverence and godly reverence"? Godly fear means more than just reverence alone—it means "to reverence with dread." As the Holy Spirit said through Isaiah the prophet:

Sanctify the LORD of hosts himself; and *let him be your fear, and let him be your dread* (Isaiah 8:13, emphasis added).

The fear of the Lord has sanctifying power. It stimulates people to "hate evil" and "depart from evil" (Prov. 3:7; 8:13). It motivates us to walk circumspectly before a holy God. Just as Paul said in 2 Corinthians 7:1:

Having therefore these promises, dearly beloved, let us cleanse ourselves from all filthiness of the flesh and spirit, *perfecting holiness in the fear of God* (emphasis added).

How do we know if we possess a true fear of God? If we had a full revelation of the true fear of God in our hearts, we would be afraid to move! The thought of our God being a "consuming fire" (Heb. 12:29) would fill us with dread. The true fear of God is what Moses and the Israelites experienced at Mount Sinai. They trembled at God's presence. We read in Hebrews 12:21, "And so terrible was the sight, that Moses said, 'I exceedingly fear and quake.'"

Some might question, "How could we ever 'come boldly to the throne of grace' if we possess such a dreadful fear of the Lord?" Only through understanding the cleansing power of Jesus' blood, which has made us righteous in God's sight, can we gain the boldness to approach our holy God. Through the substitutionary sacrifice of Jesus, God is able to present us "faultless before the presence of his glory with exceeding joy" (Jude 1:24).

Does the fear of God cause you to tremble? Consider the following scriptures:

> Serve the LORD with fear, and rejoice with *trembling* (Psalm 2:11, emphasis added).

> The LORD reigneth; let the people *tremble* (Psalm 99:1, emphasis added).

> *Tremble*, thou earth, at the presence of the Lord, at the presence of the God of Jacob (Psalm 114:7, emphasis added).

> "Fear ye not me?" saith the LORD: "will ye not *tremble* at my presence?" (Jer. 5:22, emphasis added).

> But the LORD is the true God, he is the living God, and an everlasting king: at his wrath the earth shall *tremble*, and the nations shall not be able to abide his indignation (Jer. 10:10, emphasis added).

> Wherefore, my beloved, as ye have always obeyed, not as in my presence only, but now much more in my absence, work out your own salvation with fear and *trembling* (Phil. 2:12, emphasis added).

> Thou believest that there is one God; thou doest well: the devils also believe, and *tremble* (James 2:19, emphasis added).

Many Christians have convinced themselves that there is no reason to fear a loving God; certainly He would never kill anybody or send anyone to an eternal hell. Yet Jesus wanted His friends to understand that God *does* kill, and He *does* cast people into hell. Yet many modern preachers disagree. They preach that Satan is the one who kills people and casts them into hell.

Preaching on hell is very rare in our day. Many of the ministers who do occasionally mention it are so afraid of offending someone that they preface and conclude their brief statements with apologies. Why is this so? Does hell really exist? Are sinners actually confined to suffer there for eternity?

Jesus spoke of hell and judgment very frequently. He could be considered the greatest "hell fire and brimstone" preacher of all time, one who repeatedly warned His listeners of eternal damnation using vivid detail. He described hell as a place of "torment" (Luke 16:28) where "there shall be weeping and gnashing of teeth" (Matt. 24:51). He called it "outer darkness" (Matt. 8:12) and a "furnace of fire" (Matt. 13:49-50), a place of "everlasting fire" (Matt. 25:41), and "everlasting punishment" (Matt. 25:46). The account contained in the four Gospels records Jesus describing heaven only once (see John 14), but describing hell no less than fourteen distinct times.

Some think that hell, wrath and judgment should not be mentioned in their preaching as it might cause their listeners to suffer unnecessary fear. But God wants people to fear His holy wrath! In the New Testament, hell, God's wrath and His judgment are either referred to or described at least 234 times. With that much priority given to the subject, we ought not to consider it insignificant.

The famous "faith" chapter, Hebrews 11, offers us a clear example of how fear can motivate us to obey God. Verse 7 says,

> By faith Noah, being warned of God of things not seen as yet, *moved with fear*, prepared an ark to the saving of his house; by the which he condemned the world, and became heir of the righteousness which is by faith (Heb. 11:7, emphasis added.)

Noah feared God and the "wrath to come." Being "moved with fear," his faith went into action. Today we have a society that needs to be "moved with fear," otherwise they'll be condemned to hell. We, like John the Baptist, need to warn men and women to "flee the wrath to come" (Luke 3:7). God's spokesmen have always done so in the past. Enoch (see Jude 14-15), Noah (see 2 Pet. 2:5), Moses (Deut. 32:35); the psalmists and prophets (see for example, Isaiah 24-34), the apostles, the great preachers, evangelists and reformers who have won souls down through the centuries—such as the Puritans, Wesley, Edwards, Whitefield, Finney, Spurgeon, Moody—all have faithfully proclaimed humanity's guilt, the coming judgment and the wrath of God upon the impenitent and unbelieving.

One of the most well-known sermons ever preached in America is Jonathan Edwards' *Sinners in the Hands of an Angry God*. Preached in 1741, his message is another testimony to the impact sermons about God's wrath can have. It sparked one of the greatest revivals America has seen. Here's a small portion of that message:

> The wrath of God is like great waters that are restrained for the present; but they increase more and more, and rise higher and higher, till an outlet is given; and the

longer the stream is stopped, the more rapid and mighty is its course when once it is let loose.

It is true that judgment against your evil works has not been executed hitherto; the floods of God's vengeance have been withheld, but your guilt in the meantime is constantly increasing, and you are every day treasuring up more wrath. The waters are constantly rising and waxing more and more mighty; nothing but the mere pleasure of God holds the waters back that are unwilling to be stopped, and press hard to go forward. If God should only withdraw His hand from the floodgate, it would immediately fly open, and the fiery folds of the fierceness and wrath of God would rush forth with inconceivable fury and come upon you with omnipotent power. If your strength were ten thousand times greater than it is, yea, ten thousand times greater than the strength of the stoutest, sturdiest devil in Hell, it would be nothing to withstand or endure it.

The bow of God's wrath is bent and the arrow made ready on the string. Justice directs the bow to your heart, and strains at the bow. Nothing but the mere pleasure of God—that of an angry God—without any promise or obligation at all, keeps the arrow one moment from being made drunk with your blood.

The God who holds you over the pit of Hell much in the same way as one holds a spider or some loathsome insect over the fire, abhors you and is dreadfully provoked. His wrath toward you burns like fire. He looks upon you as worthy of nothing else but to be cast into the fire. He is of purer eyes than to bear to have you in His sight. You are ten thousand times more abominable in His eyes than the most hateful venomous serpent is in ours. You have offended Him infinitely more than ever a stubborn rebel did his prince; yet, it is nothing but His hand that holds you from falling into the fire every moment.

Does this sound like anything we've heard in our pulpits in recent years? Today we are reminded so often of God's love for us that we wouldn't think of sitting through such a sermon. Ironically, those present at Jonathan Edwards' message weren't sitting either, because many fell to the floor, crying out to God for mercy! That solitary sermon sent shock waves of revival throughout New England.

Another powerful American revival began under the ministry of Charles Finney in the early 1800s. Finney witnessed over two-and-a-half million conversions under his ministry during an era long before radio and TV existed. Finney had no flashy promotion. He simply preached a biblical gospel with a heart of devotion. Reflecting on one of the greatest moves of God he saw, Finney wrote,

> That night I determined that I would cry aloud against the sins of the people and bring to bear the very fires of hell as a final consequence of their rebellion. For almost two hours I literally flailed the evildoers who sat before me. I called God to witness that the judgment was not far off for them. Concluding, I gave a few moments to the mercy of God but I did that in a stern manner. I was determined that the people should for once stand face-to-face with the fact of sin and hell. That night the meeting broke and I think I never experienced such a divine demonstration.[1]

No true servant of God would want to gloss over the truth of hell and impending judgment. Jesus set the pattern for all

---

[1]As quoted in *Sin's Explosion*, Jack Van Impe, p. 224

of us, preaching "the truth in love," and faithful spokespersons of God have followed His example down through history. The great soul winner, evangelist Billy Sunday, once said,

> I would rather believe and preach a truth, no matter how unpleasant it is, than to believe and preach a pleasant lie. I believe there is a hell. If I didn't, I wouldn't have the audacity to stand up here and preach to you.[2]

Where are the Jonathan Edwardses, Charles Finneys and Billy Sundays today?

---

[2] *Great Preaching on Hell*, pp. 124-25

THREE

God is a Killer

God judgeth the righteous, and God is angry with the wicked every day. If he turn not, he will whet [sharpen] his sword; he hath bent his bow, and made it ready. He hath also prepared for him the instruments of death; he ordaineth his arrows against the persecutors (Psalm 7:11-13).

And my wrath shall wax hot, and I will kill you with the sword; and your wives shall be widows, and your children fatherless (Ex. 22:24).

See now that I, even I, am he, and there is no god with me: I kill, and I make alive; I wound, and I heal: neither is there any that can deliver out of my hand (Deut. 32:39).

The LORD killeth, and maketh alive: he bringeth down to the grave, and bringeth up (1 Samuel 2:6).

And I gave her space to repent of her fornication; and she

*repented not. Behold, I will cast her into a bed, and them
that commit adultery with her into great tribulation,
except they repent of their deeds. And I will kill her children with death; and all the churches shall know that I am
he which searcheth the reins and hearts: and I will give
unto every one of you according to your works*
(Rev. 2:21-23).

The thought that God is a killer makes some people recoil
with unbelief. But the truth stands: God is a killer, and
the above scriptures and many similar ones prove it.

The very fact that Satan lied to Adam and Eve, telling
them, "Ye shall not surely die" (Gen. 3:4), reveals to us the
one who wants to deny this vital biblical truth. The Lord
warned Adam and Eve of a judgment of death if they ate from
the tree. After they sinned, God pronounced various judgments upon them, casting them out of the garden. Our loving,
merciful God did this!

Later, the Lord stationed guardian Cherubims with a
flaming sword to guard the tree of life. This was to ensure that
humankind would not live forever, but would in fact die.
Those Cherubims and their flaming sword were not stationed
as decorations—they were instruments of death!

From that point, death was passed to all, for all have
sinned. (see Rom. 5:12). *Death proves there is judgment for
sin.* All sin and all die. But death is not just a passive or
consequential judgment. Rather, in the Bible, death is often
the direct result of God's wrath.

Yes, God does kill people, and I've compiled a list of
scriptures for your examination that clearly proves it. You

may tire of reading the list that follows and be tempted to skip to the next chapter before you finish reading them all. I encourage you, however, to read as many as you can so this truth is indelibly imprinted on your heart and mind.

In Genesis 6:17, God said during Noah's time,

> "And, behold, *I, even I*, do bring a flood of waters upon the earth, to destroy all flesh, wherein is the breath of life, from under heaven; and every thing that is in the earth shall die" (emphasis added).

Possibly as many as two-hundred million men, women, boys and girls died as a result of this one act of God's judgment. All human life perished, and God emphatically stated that He brought the flood upon the earth.

In Genesis 19:24-25 we read,

> "Then the LORD rained upon Sodom and upon Gomorrah brimstone and fire from the LORD out of heaven; And he overthrew those cities, and all the plain, and all the inhabitants of the cities, and that which grew upon the ground."

God did it, not Satan. This was not a freak act of nature as some Bible commentators claim. The apostle Peter said that particular judgment served as an example of God's wrath. (see 2 Peter 2:6).

In Genesis 20:3-7, God warned King Abimelech that he would be a dead man if he didn't give Sarah back to her husband, Abraham. His fear of God's judgment motivated him to respond immediately.

We read in Genesis 38:7-10,

And Er, Judah's firstborn, was wicked in the sight of the LORD; and *the LORD slew him.* And Judah said unto Onan, "Go in unto thy brother's wife, and marry her, and raise up seed to thy brother." And Onan knew that the seed should not be his; and it came to pass, when he went in unto his brother's wife, that he spilled it on the ground, lest that he should give seed to his brother. And the thing which he did displeased the LORD: wherefore *He slew him also* (emphasis added).

In Exodus 4:21-23, God told Moses to inform Pharaoh to release His people or He would kill Pharaoh's firstborn son. This was no idle threat:

"And it came to pass, that at midnight *the LORD smote all the firstborn* in the land of Egypt, from the firstborn of Pharaoh that sat on his throne unto the firstborn of the captive that was in the dungeon; and all the firstborn of cattle. And Pharaoh rose up in the night, he, and all his servants, and all the Egyptians; and there was a great cry in Egypt; for there was not a house where there was not one dead" (Ex. 12:29-30, emphasis added).

In Exodus 4:24, Moses failed to circumcise his son, and "the LORD met him, and *sought to kill him*" (emphasis added).

In Exodus 14:24-28, God caused the wheels to fall off the Egyptian chariots, dooming the army to drown as He caused the Red Sea to fall back upon them.

Exodus 14:30-31 states,

"Thus the LORD saved Israel that day out of the hand of the Egyptians; and Israel saw the Egyptians dead upon the sea shore. And Israel saw that great work which *the LORD did* upon the Egyptians: and the people feared the LORD, and believed the LORD, and his servant Moses" (emphasis added).

In Exodus 22:22-24, God warned that if an Israelite abused any widow or fatherless child, He would kill that person, promising that his wife would become a widow, and his children, fatherless.

Exodus 32:35 says,

"And the LORD plagued the people, because they made the calf...and many died by the plague."

In Leviticus 10:1-2, the two sons of Aaron, Nadab and Abihu, were killed by God when they offered "strange fire."

In Numbers 11:1-3, God sent fire and incinerated many people for their constant complaining.

In Numbers 11:31-33, because the Israelites complained about eating manna, God sent them great flocks of quail to eat. The people spent an entire night and day collecting them. However, in 11:33 we read, "the wrath of the LORD was kindled against the people, and the LORD smote the people with a very great plague, and they died."

In Numbers 14:12, because of Israel's unbelief and refusal to enter into the promised land, God said, "I will smite them with the pestilence." In 14:36-37 we read,

"And the men, which Moses sent to search the land, who returned, and made all the congregation to murmur against him, by bringing up a slander upon the land, even those men that did bring up the evil report upon the land, died by the plague before the LORD."

The remaining adults all died in the wilderness for their sin of unbelief.

In Numbers 16:31-34, God caused the earth to open up and swallow a man named Korah, his family and followers for their rebellion against Moses.

In Numbers 16:35, "fire from the Lord" came down and "consumed the two hundred and fifty men" who joined Korah's rebellion. I seriously doubt that any in that group deny the fact that God kills people.

In Numbers 16:41-49, God sent a plague on those who murmured about Korah and his family, and in a short time 14,700 people died.

In Numbers 21:4-6, while the children of Israel journeyed from Mount Hor, they "spake against God, and against Moses," complaining about leaving Egypt and having to eat God's miracle bread. Verse 6 says, "And *the LORD sent fiery serpents among the people*, and they bit the people; and much people of Israel died" (emphasis added).

In Numbers 22:22-33, we read that "God's anger was kindled" against Balaam because of his many acts of disobedience. Verse 33 states that the angel of the Lord would have killed him had he continued on his path of rebellion. His stubborn donkey saved his life.

In Numbers 25:1-9, once again "the anger of the Lord was kindled against Israel" (25:3) for their idolatry and sexual sins. A plague was sent from God that killed 24,000 people.

In Deuteronomy 2:21-22, God destroyed an entire group of people.

In Joshua 10:10-11, God sent a strong hailstorm, killing hundreds of men in battle.

In Judges 20:35, "the Lord smote" the armies of Benjamin, resulting in the death of 25,100 soldiers.

In 1 Samuel 2:6-7, Hannah prophesied,

> *"The LORD killeth, and maketh alive: he bringeth down to the grave, and bringeth up"* (emphasis added).

In 1 Samuel 5:6-9, the Lord struck the Philistines with tumors for stealing the ark of God. Verses 11-12 state,

> So they sent and gathered together all the lords of the Philistines, and said, "Send away the ark of the God of Israel, and let it go again to his own place, that it slay us not, and our people": for there was a deadly destruction throughout all the city; the hand of God was very heavy there. And the men that died not were smitten with the emerods: and the cry of the city went up to heaven.

In 1 Samuel 6:19, seventy men were killed for looking inside the ark of God.

In 1 Samuel 25:36-38, ungrateful Nabal's "heart died within him," and ten days later "the Lord smote Nabal, so that he died."

In 2 Samuel 6:7, we read that the "anger of the Lord was kindled against Uzzah, and God smote him there for his error; and there he died by the ark of God."

After David committed adultery with Bathsheba and had her husband killed, Nathan the prophet told David in 2 Samuel 12:10-15,

"'Now therefore the sword shall never depart from thine house; because thou hast despised Me, and hast taken the wife of Uriah the Hittite to be thy wife.' Thus saith the LORD, 'Behold, I will raise up evil against thee out of thine own house, and I will take thy wives before thine eyes, and give them unto thy neighbour, and he shall lie with thy wives in the sight of this sun. For thou didst it secretly: but I will do this thing before all Israel, and before the sun.'" And David said unto Nathan, "I have sinned against the LORD." And Nathan said unto David, "The LORD also hath put away thy sin; thou shalt not die. Howbeit, because by this deed thou hast given great occasion to the enemies of the LORD to blaspheme, the child also that is born unto thee shall surely die." And Nathan departed unto his house. And the LORD struck the child that Uriah's wife bare unto David, and it was very sick.

As you probably know, the baby died a short time later. God's Word warns us all in Hebrews 13:4,

"Marriage is honourable in all, and the bed undefiled: but whoremongers and adulterers God will judge."

In 2 Samuel 24:12-16, David, once more facing God's wrath, was given a choice of three judgments: either seven years of famine, three months of being chased by his enemies, or three days of pestilence in the land. He chose the plague and 70,000 people died.

In 1 Kings 13:7-28, a prophet was killed by a lion because he disobeyed the word of the Lord. Verse 26 says, "Therefore the LORD hath delivered him unto the lion, which hath torn him, and slain him, according to the word of the LORD, which he spake unto him."

In 1 Kings 14:1-17, King Jeroboam's son was struck with sickness, and God refused to heal him.

In 1 Kings 20:35-36, a man who refused to obey the son of a prophet and the word of the Lord was attacked and killed by a lion because of his disobedience.

In 1 Kings 21:19-25, Elijah pronounced judgment against King Ahab and his wife Jezebel for having Naboth stoned. He stated that the dogs would lick up King Ahab's blood in the exact same place the dogs licked up Naboth's blood, and dogs would eat Jezebel's body along with their children.

In 1 Kings 22:19-38, God sent a lying spirit to some false prophets to persuade King Ahab to go into battle so he would be killed. During the battle, a random arrow struck King Ahab in the side, killing him. Afterwards, they washed his blood from his chariot and the dogs licked it up, fulfilling the word of the Lord through Elijah.

In 2 Kings 1:9-14, fifty-two men were consumed by fire before the Lord as they came to take Elijah forcibly away.

In 2 Kings 2:23-24, forty-two young men were mauled by female bears for mocking Elisha.

In 2 Kings 7:1-2, Elisha pronounced judgment on an unbelieving man for mocking the word of the Lord. In 7:16-20, we read that he was trampled to death the very next day.

In 2 Kings 9:30-37, the word of the Lord against Jezebel was fulfilled as she was thrown down and killed.

In 2 Kings 15:5, King Azariah was struck with leprosy and died for his sin of pride and rebellion.

In 2 Kings 17:25, God sent lions that attacked and killed

men who refused to fear God.

In 2 Kings 19:34-35, 185,000 Assyrians were killed in one night by an angel of the Lord.

In 2 Chronicles 13:15,20, God smote Jeroboam so that he died.

In 2 Chronicles 14:12-13, God smote the Ethiopians and they "could not recover themselves: for they were destroyed before the Lord."

In 2 Chronicles 20:22-24, God set ambushments against three enemy armies and they slew one another so that there were "dead bodies fallen to the earth, and none escaped."

In 2 Chronicles 21:11-15, Elijah wrote a letter to King Jehoram and his people, telling them that because of their sexual sins, He would smite them with a great plague. (Why are so many Christians today so quick to deny God's judgment in the outbreak of sexual diseases?)

2 Chronicles 21:18-19 says,

> "And after all this *the LORD smote him in his bowels with an incurable disease.* And it came to pass, that in process of time, after the end of two years, his bowels fell out by reason of his sickness: so he died of sore [terrible] diseases" (emphasis added).

In 2 Chronicles 26:16-21, King Uzziah was struck with leprosy for his pride, and God refused to heal him, so he died.

In 2 Chronicles 36:15-21, we read that Israel mocked, despised and misused the prophets "until the wrath of the Lord arose against his people, till there was no remedy." Consequently, an enemy nation invaded and slew the young men right in their sanctuary. Young and old were killed.

38

Nearly all the prophets thundered the truth that God is a killer.

In Jeremiah 21:5-6, God said,

> "And I myself will fight against you with an outstretched hand and with a strong arm, even in anger, and in fury, and in great wrath. And I will smite the inhabitants of this city, both man and beast: they shall die of a great pestilence."

In Jeremiah 28:15-17, Jeremiah prophesied against the false prophet Hananiah, telling him he would die that year for giving a false message. He died that same year in the seventh month.

In Jeremiah 33:5, God said He would fill the place with "the dead bodies of men, whom I have slain in mine anger and in my fury, and for all whose wickedness I have hid my face from this city."

Ezekiel 6:12 says,

> "He that is far off shall die of the pestilence; and he that is near shall fall by the sword; and he that remaineth and is besieged shall die by the famine: thus will I accomplish my fury upon them."

In Ezekiel 14:21, God pronounced judgment on His chosen people, saying,

> "For thus saith the Lord GOD; 'How much more when I send my four sore judgments upon Jerusalem, the sword, and the famine, and the noisome beast, and the pestilence, to cut off from it man and beast?'"

Believe it or not, I have not come close to exhausting the

numerous scriptures that could be listed, proving God is a killer. We could continue on for many pages. My dear friend, it is about time we allow God to be who He says He is. We must face up to the fact that "it is a fearful thing to fall into the hands of the living God" (Heb. 10:31) Is your God a killer? If He's not, then your god is not the God of the Bible.

FOUR

But That's the Old Testament!

Behold therefore the goodness and severity of God: on them which fell, severity; but toward thee, goodness, if thou continue in His goodness: otherwise thou also shalt be cut off (Rom. 11:22).

One of the most absurd notions that has been swallowed by many modern Christians is that we shouldn't take anyone seriously who quotes from the Old Testament. How often have you heard the objection, "But that's from the Old Testament," as if the Old Testament is an uninspired portion of God's Word?

The fact is that the Old Testament was the only Bible from which Jesus preached, and it was the only Bible the early Christians had. Peter quoted from the Old Testament in his sermon on the day of Pentecost, and three thousand people were saved. Philip preached Christ from the Old Testament book of Isaiah to an Ethiopian eunuch who consequently was born again. When teaching in the synagogues to Jews, Paul used the Old Testament to convince them that Jesus was indeed the Christ.

Writing to Timothy, Paul said, "All Scripture is given by inspiration of God, and is profitable for doctrine, for reproof, for correction, for instruction in righteousness" (2 Timothy 3:16). *All* Scripture is God-breathed, thus the Old Testament as well as the New is "profitable for doctrine." Practically any Bible doctrine can be proved from the Old Testament. For example, God's grace is found there. In Genesis 6:8 we read that "Noah found grace in the eyes of the Lord." Justification by faith is also an Old Testament doctrine. Habakkuk wrote that "the just shall live by faith" (Hab. 2:4).

The Old Testament is the Word of God, thus it is eternal. It is every bit as inspired as the New Testament, because the Holy Spirit inspired those who wrote it. Speaking of the Old Testament, Peter wrote that "holy men of God spake as they were moved by the Holy Ghost" (2 Peter 1:21).

The difference between the Old and New is quite simple. The Old Testament contains the testament or "agreement" between God and Israel through the Law, and the New Testament gives us a "better testament" (Heb. 7:22) through Christ. This is not to say, however, that God's character has changed. This is clear from the following verses:

> They shall perish, but thou shalt endure: yea, all of them shall wax old like a garment; as a vesture shalt thou change them, and they shall be changed: But *thou art the same*, and thy years shall have no end (Psalm 102:26-27, emphasis added).

> "For I am the LORD, *I change not*" (Mal 3:6, emphasis added).

Jesus Christ the same yesterday, and today, and for ever (Heb. 13:8).

Every good gift and every perfect gift is from above, and cometh down from the Father of lights, *with whom is no variableness, neither shadow of turning* (James 1:17, emphasis added).

God never needs to change because He's perfect. Perfection never needs to be updated or improved. God's character now is the same as it was during the time of the Old Testament. Some think of Him as being more severe and easily angered under the Old Testament, but more kind and loving under the New. What an absurd idea! Thank God He has never changed!

The fact is, we do ourselves a disservice by rejecting Old Testament revelations of the Lord, because some of the most revealing statements of His graciousness, mercy, compassion, kindness, gentleness and long-suffering are found there. Verse after verse reminds us of His wonderful character.

Let's examine how God once described Himself to Moses:

And the LORD descended in the cloud, and stood with him there, and proclaimed the name of the LORD. And the LORD passed by before him, and proclaimed, "The LORD, The LORD God, merciful and gracious, long-suffering, and abundant in goodness and truth, keeping mercy for thousands, forgiving iniquity and transgression and sin, and that will by no means clear the guilty; visiting the iniquity of the fathers upon the children, and upon the children's children, unto the third and to the fourth generation" (Ex. 34:5-7).

What a beautiful glimpse of our heavenly Father! If this was the only passage in the Bible that revealed God to us, we would know of both His love and wrath. Sin is the only thing God hates. He does not hate poor people or rich people, dumb people or smart people, talented people or untalented people. He only hates sin, and sin inevitably invites His wrath because He is holy and just. *This will never change, because it is the character of the perfect One!*

Is the God of the Old Testament a jealous God? Yes, (see Exodus 20:5) and so is the God of the New Testament: "Do we provoke the Lord to jealousy?" (1 Cor. 10:22).

Is the God of the Old Testament a God of vengeance? Certainly, and so is the God of the New Testament: "Vengeance is mine; I will repay" (Rom. 12:19; Heb. 10:30). "In flaming fire taking vengeance on them" (2 Thes. 1:8).

Did the Old Testament demand death without mercy for the sinner? Yes, but the New Testament says, "Of how much sorer punishment, suppose ye, shall he be thought worthy, who hath trodden under foot the Son of God" (Heb. 10:29).

Does the God of the Old Testament dispatch lying spirits to deceive the wicked? Again, yes, and so does the God of the New Testament. Paul said, "God shall send them strong delusion, that they should believe a lie: That they all might be damned who believed not the truth, but had pleasure in unrighteousness" (2 Thes. 2:11-12.)

Did God threaten people with curses in the Old Testament? He still does in the New: "But though we, or an angel from heaven, preach any other gospel unto you than that which we have preached unto you, let him be accursed" (Gal. 1:8), and "If any man love not the Lord Jesus Christ, let him be Anathema [cursed]" (1 Cor. 16:22).

Under the new agreement of the New Testament, God's ways have not changed. He is just as merciful and compassionate and just as holy and wrathful. Let's look at some New Testament examples of His anger and wrath. Again, you may be tempted to just read a few of the following examples, but I encourage you to read them all. That way, you'll be completely convinced.

In Matthew 21:18-19, Jesus cursed a fruit tree, causing it to wither up from its roots. It never again bore fruit. Incidentally, this was not the first time we read of God cursing plant life or destroying crops. This is the same great I AM that cursed the ground in Genesis 3 and chased Adam and Eve out of the garden.

In Luke 1:20, Zechariah, the father of John the Baptist was struck with muteness because of his sin of unbelief. He remained that way for nearly a year.

Years later, Zechariah's prophet-son preached on the wrath of God:

> Then said he to the multitude that came forth to be baptized of him, "O generation of vipers, who hath warned you to flee from the wrath to come?" (Luke 3:7).

In Luke 13:1-5 Jesus referred to some contemporary, tragic deaths that had occurred. Some people had been murdered, and others had been killed in a freak accident. Jesus told His audience not to think of themselves as better than those who died, but warned them that if they did not repent, they would "all likewise perish."

Recorded in all four Gospels is the story of Jesus chasing people out of the temple with a whip. No one can intelligently argue that Jesus was not demonstrating God's wrath as He "poured out the changers' money, and overthrew the tables" as well as "the seats of them that sold doves." As He did, He quoted from Jeremiah 7:11, a seething chapter on God's wrath.

In John 5:1-15, a certain man who had suffered with an infirmity for thirty-eight years was healed instantly by Jesus. It is interesting to note, however, that in 5:14, Jesus told the man, "Behold, thou art made whole: sin no more, *lest a worse thing come unto thee*" (emphasis added). Obviously, sickness can sometimes be a direct result of sin.

We shouldn't conclude, however, that every sickness is an indication of sin in a person's life. We read in John's Gospel of Jesus healing a man who had been born blind. When asked by His disciples whose sin had caused the man's blindness, his or his parents', Jesus replied, "Neither hath this man sinned, nor his parents: but that the works of God should be made manifest in him" (John 9:3). So sin was not the reason for the man's blindness. In the same way, not every time someone is sick should we automatically conclude that it is the result of sin. On the other hand, we should also be careful not to dismiss the possibility that some needing healing may first need to repent of some sin before they will be healed.

There are other New Testament examples of the connection between sin and sickness. Jesus once said to a paralytic just before He healed him, "Thy sins be forgiven thee" (Matthew 9:2). Apparently sin was an issue in his case. Yet in every other instance when Jesus healed paralytics, either personally or through an apostle, sin was never mentioned (see Matthew 4:24; 8:6-7; Acts 8:7; 9:33-34).

The apostle James connected sin and sickness when he said,

"Is any sick among you? Let him call for the elders of the church; and let them pray over him, anointing him with oil in the name of the Lord: And the prayer of faith shall save the sick, and the Lord shall raise him up; and *if he has committed sins, they shall be forgiven him*" (James 5:14-15, emphasis added).

The apostle Paul likewise gives us reason to believe that Christians might become sick because of unconfessed sin in their lives. He states in 1 Corinthians 11:27-32 that some of the Corinthians were being "chastened of the Lord" and consequently were "weak and sickly." Some had even died for neglecting to judge themselves (that is, confess and repent of their sins) before taking the Lord's Supper. Naturally, God chastens only the disobedient, not the obedient.

Paul wrote,

"For if we would judge ourselves, we should not be judged. But when we are judged, we are chastened of the Lord, that we should not be condemned with the world" (1 Cor. 11:31-32).

This is vital for us to understand. Many of the Corinthians were involved in strife and carnality, and were even getting drunk and committing sexual sins. Paul warned them that if they would not judge themselves they would be judged! Either we deal with our sin or God will deal with it. And, according to Paul, God might deal with it by means of weakness, sickness or sometimes even death. Our churches need to recognize this truth.

In Acts 5:1-11, Ananias and Sapphira conspired in an attempt to impress the church concerning a financial donation. According to Scripture they were guilty of lying to the Holy Ghost, and both were struck dead. The result was that "great fear came upon all the church, and upon as many as heard these things." It's significant to notice that nearly every time the fear of God is mentioned in Acts, great signs and wonders are also mentioned. Could this be one reason why we are seeing so few miracles in our day?

In Acts 9:8-9, Saul, who later became the apostle Paul, was knocked to the ground and struck with blindness for three days. He began his relationship with God by experiencing God's discipline.

In Acts 12:23, King Herod, who had just killed the apostle James, refused to give honor to God and was struck down and ultimately died, diseased with maggots.

In Acts 13:6-12, Elymas, a false prophet, was struck with blindness for withstanding the ministry of Paul and Barnabas.

In Romans 1:18, Paul said,

> "For the wrath of God is revealed from heaven against all ungodliness and unrighteousness of men, who hold the truth in unrighteousness."

In Romans 9:22, Paul stated that God makes His power known by showing His wrath.

In 1 Corinthians 3:17, Paul declared

> "If any man defile the temple of God, him shall God destroy; for the temple of God is holy, which temple ye are."

In Ephesians 5:6, we're warned to not allow anyone to deceive us into believing that God's wrath will not come upon those who practice sexual sins and covetousness.

In Colossians 3:5-6, we're again warned to shun sexual sins, greediness and idolatry in our lives, or the wrath of God will come upon us for our disobedience.

In Hebrews 10:26-31, we are solemnly informed that if we sin willfully by renouncing Christ, despising the gospel, treading the Son of God under our feet, counting His blood as an unholy thing and insulting the Holy Spirit, there remains no sacrifice for our sins, but a certain fearful judgment, fiery indignation and revenge from the Lord. For "it is a fearful thing to fall into the hands of the living God."

In Revelation, one chapter after another reveals the wrath of God being poured out upon the ungodly. We read of war, famine, death, earthquakes, hail, fire, the sea turning to blood, water becoming poisoned, demon locusts harassing humanity, grievous sores breaking out, scorching heat, darkness and fire from heaven. These are all direct acts of God.

Christians often associate wrath with God the Father and love with Jesus the Son. But notice that John wrote of the wrath of *the Lamb*, a wrath that terrifies the earth's inhabitants. Jesus is that Lamb:

> And the kings of the earth, and the great men, and the rich men, and the chief captains, and the mighty men, and every bondman, and every free man, hid themselves in the dens and in the rocks of the mountains; And said to the mountains and rocks, Fall on us, and hide us from the face of him that sitteth on the throne, and from the wrath of the Lamb: For the great day of his wrath is come; and who shall be able to stand? (Rev. 6:15-17).

Finally, let's read John's description of hell, a place described as being "in the presence of the Lamb," the ultimate example of God's wrath:

> And the third angel followed them, saying with a loud

voice, "If any man worship the beast and his image, and receive his mark in his forehead, or in his hand, the same shall drink of the wine of the wrath of God, which is poured out without mixture into the cup of his indignation; and he shall be tormented with fire and brimstone in the presence of the holy angels, and in the presence of the Lamb: And the smoke of their torment ascendeth up for ever and ever: and they have no rest day nor night, who worship the beast and his image, and whosoever receiveth the mark of his name" (Rev. 14:9-11).

The entire New Testament is filled with examples of God's pouring out His wrath. Let it be settled in your mind once and for all that God is never going to change because He is perfect. We are the ones who must change, and if we don't, we must stand judged by His unchanging standards of holiness!

The closing warning of Revelation 22:18-19 plainly states that if you add to God's Word, then God "shall add unto him the plagues that are written in this book," and if you take away from God's Word, God "shall take away [your] part out of the book of life, and out of the holy city, and from the things which are written in this book." What stronger New Testament example do we need to verify the fact that God is the same, yesterday, today and forever? He is a God of wrath!

Indeed, the New Testament has an abundance to say about God's wrath and judgment. Forget the preposterous notion that God has changed under the New Testament. His attitude toward rebellion and sin has never changed. God feels the same today about sin as He always has. Thank God He is a gracious Lord, ready and willing to forgive all who will repent!

FIVE

But God Wouldn't Do That!

God thundereth marvelously with his voice; great things doeth he, which we cannot comprehend....Touching the Almighty, we cannot find him out: he is excellent in power, and in judgment (Job 37:5,23).

As thou knowest not what is the way of the spirit, nor how the bones do grow in the womb of her that is with child: even so thou knowest not the works of God who maketh all (Ecc. 11:5).

For my thoughts are not your thoughts, neither are your ways my ways, saith the LORD. For as the heavens are higher than the earth, so are my ways higher than your ways, and my thoughts than your thoughts (Is. 55:8-9).

O the depth of the riches both of the wisdom and knowledge of God! how unsearchable are his judgments, and his ways past finding out! For who hath known the mind of the Lord? or who hath been his counsellor? (Rom. 11:33-34).

Why dost thou strive against him? for he giveth not account of any of his matters (Job 33:13).

God needs to answer to no one. As the above scriptures so clearly indicate, He can do anything He chooses, and He will always do what is consistent with His character. Without exception, His deeds are done in righteousness, because He is righteous.

When I preach that God sometimes kills and destroys, some Christians object, simply because they've created a God in their own image. Many don't want a God who is "angry with the wicked every day" as the Bible states our God is (Psalm 7:11); they prefer a heavenly Santa Claus, a jovial type whose only business is to bless.

We must be mature enough to accept everything the Bible says about God. It is wrong for us to play "pick and choose" with Bible verses. Let's choose them all. For example, let us believe that God is the healer, but let us also recognize Him as one who brings afflictions. King David did:

> "I know, O LORD, that thy judgments are right, and that thou in faithfulness hast afflicted me" (Psalm 119:75).

It's obvious from reading this same psalm that David understood God's righteous purpose in disciplining him. He said,

> "Before I was afflicted I went astray: but now have I kept thy word....It is good for me that I have been afflicted; that I might learn thy statutes" (Psalm 119:67,71).

No matter how much we may want to deny it, God chastises and disciplines the disobedient. Do you recognize Him as that kind of God? The great prophet Jeremiah did. He said,

> "I am the man that hath seen affliction by the rod of his wrath" (Lam. 3:1).

The prophet Isaiah agreed:

> "For my name's sake will I defer mine anger, and for my praise will I refrain for thee, that I cut thee not off. Behold, I have refined thee, but not with silver; I have chosen thee in the furnace of affliction. For mine own sake, even for mine own sake, will I do it: for how should my name be polluted? and I will not give my glory unto another" (Is. 48:9-11).

Solomon wrote of a loving God who sometimes chastens His own:

> My son, despise not the chastening of the LORD; neither be weary of his correction: For whom the LORD loveth he correcteth; even as a father the son in whom he delighteth (Prov. 3:11-12).

Moses saw this aspect of God's character and challenged us to consider it in our hearts:

> Thou shalt also consider in thine heart, that, as a man chasteneth his son, so the LORD thy God chasteneth thee (Deut. 8:5).

In God's great wisdom, He sometimes chooses to rock our boats to produce His desired results in our lives. The writer of Hebrews tells us exactly why God chastens us:

Furthermore we have had fathers of our flesh which corrected us, and we gave them reverence: shall we not much rather be in subjection unto the Father of spirits, and live? For they verily for a few days chastened us after their own pleasure; but he for our profit, that we might be partakers of his holiness. Now no chastening for the present seemeth to be joyous, but grievous: nevertheless afterward it yieldeth the peaceable fruit of righteousness unto them which are exercised thereby (Heb. 12:9-11).

God's corrective judgment is meant not only to reveal His displeasure of our sin, but to also produce His holiness in our lives. God's wrath is never hasty or erratic; His anger is always directed at disobedience. This might be difficult for those of us who are parents to understand because we often are inconsistent in disciplining our children. Sometimes we go overboard in correcting them and at other times we let them "get away with murder." The Lord, however, is never that way. He's always consistent. In fact, the writer of Hebrews said that if we aren't periodically disciplined by God, that proves we aren't one of His children (see Heb. 12:7-8).

Although we may not always recognize God's hand of discipline, He always punishes unrepentant sin. Thank God for His longsuffering, but if we continue in our selfish ways, our sin will find us out as God warns us in Numbers 32:23.

As you read the following examples of God doing things that many Christians don't think He does, remember that they were always done in righteousness, most of them being judgments on pride, rebellion or some other type of disobedience. Once again, I encourage you to read them all. (This list is not quite as long as the previous lists you've read.)

In Genesis 11:7-9, we read how God caused the mass confusion of a multitude of people by "confounding the language of all the earth." There is still confusion in the world today because of this ancient act of God, and it should serve as a continual reminder to humanity that God is a righteous judge.

In Genesis 12:3, we read of God saying to Abram, "And I will bless them that bless thee, and curse him that curseth thee." God declared that He would curse some people! In verse 17 of the same chapter, we read of Pharaoh taking Sarai into his own house, "And the LORD plagued Pharaoh and his house with great plagues because of Sarai Abram's wife." *God* did it! Who are we to say that God does not curse people or afflict them with disease?

In Genesis 19:11, two angels entered into Sodom and smote hundreds of men and boys with total blindness because of their perversion.

In Genesis 20:17-18, Abraham prayed for King Abimelech, his wife and his maidservants to be healed of barrenness, because "the LORD had fast closed up all the wombs of the house of Abimelech, because of Sarah Abraham's wife." Who are we to say God wouldn't do such a thing when the Scripture plainly says He does?

In Genesis 32:25, the Lord appeared to Jacob, and by simply touching "the hollow of Jacob's thigh," forced it out of joint, which made him limp.

In Exodus 4:11, God asked Moses a question, one that requires preachers to perform exegetical gymnastics who attempt to explain it away:

"Who hath made man's mouth? or who maketh the

dumb, or deaf, or the seeing, or the blind? have not I the
LORD?"

What could be meant by this verse other than its plain
meaning?

In Exodus 23:27, God said He would force people out of
their land by His fear. Verse 28 says that God would send
hornets to drive Israel's enemies out. God obviously has
control over insects and can use them to cause destruction
and pain against humankind.

Exodus 32:35 says,

> "And the LORD plagued the people, because they
> made the calf."

In Numbers 5:21, we read that an adulterer's thigh could
rot and her belly swell because of the curse of the Lord.

In Numbers 12, Miriam and Aaron self-righteously spoke
against Moses because they didn't approve of his wife.
Verses 9-10 tell us that "the anger of the Lord was kindled
against them" and Miriam was struck with leprosy. After her
repentance, Moses prayed that the Lord would heal her, yet
God refused to do so for seven days in order to humble her and
teach her a lesson. Consider this if you have spoken evil of
someone.

Deuteronomy 29:22-28 predicted that those who observed
Israel would

> "see the plagues of that land, and the sicknesses which
> the Lord hath laid upon it...in his anger, and in his
> wrath....And the anger of the LORD was kindled against
> this land, to bring upon it all the curses that are written

in this book: And the LORD rooted them out of their land in anger, and in wrath, and in great indignation, and cast them into another land, as it is this day."

History confirms this judgment occurred just as God promised.

In 1 Samuel 1:5, we read concerning Hannah that "the Lord had shut up her womb." Later, in answer to her prayer, she had many children.

In 1 Samuel 16:14,23; 18:10, we read that God removed His Spirit from King Saul because of his rebellion and sent "an evil spirit from the Lord" to "trouble him" with insanity.

In 1 Kings 13:1-4, God smote King Jeroboam and caused his hand to wither up when he tried to do violence to a man of God who prophesied to him. Only after repenting did God heal Jeroboam.

In 1 Kings 22;19-22, God sent a "lying spirit" in order to persuade King Ahab to go into battle to be killed.

In 2 Kings 5:20-27, Elisha's servant, Gehazi, was struck with Naaman's leprosy because of greed and lying.

In 2 Kings 6:18, the entire Syrian army was struck with blindness.

In 2 Kings 7:5-7, God frightened the Syrian army by causing them to "hear a noise of chariots, and a noise of horses, even the noise of a great host," and they fled their camps.

In 2 Kings 20:14-18, Isaiah pronounced a judgment against King Hezekiah that all his goods would be stolen and his children would be made slaves.

In 2 Chronicles 20:22-24, God set traps against three enemy armies causing them to kill one another so that there were "dead bodies fallen to the earth, and none escaped."

In 2 Chronicles 20:35-37, God pronounced judgment against King Jehoshaphat and destroyed all the new ships they had just built.

Ezra 5:12 verifies that because the children of Israel provoked God, He turned them over to an evil king, who in turn made slaves of them.

Many of the prophets warned of God's righteous acts of judgment, such as in Ezekiel 25:17:

> "And I will execute great vengeance upon them with furious rebukes; and they shall know that I am the LORD, when I shall lay my vengeance upon them."

In Daniel 4:28-37, God caused proud King Nebuchadnezzar to become insane. Consequently, he acted like an animal for seven years. Afterwards, he repented and God restored his mind.

In Micah 6:13, God said,

> "Therefore also will I make thee sick in smiting thee, in making thee desolate because of thy sins." Yes, God does make people sick!

In Malachi 2:1-3, God warned His priests,

> "And now, O ye priests, this commandment is for you. If ye will not hear, and if ye will not lay it to heart, to

give glory unto my name, saith the LORD of hosts, I will even send a curse upon you, and I will curse your blessings: yea, I have cursed them already, because ye do not lay it to heart. Behold, I will corrupt your seed, and spread dung upon your faces, even the dung of your solemn feasts; and one shall take you away with it."

Malachi went on to prophesy these powerful words in 2:17:

"Ye have wearied the LORD with your words. Yet ye say, 'Wherein have we wearied him?' When ye say, 'Every one that doeth evil is good in the sight of the LORD, and he delighteth in them'; or, 'Where is the God of judgment?'"

The books of the prophets are filled with example after example of God's hand in judgment. Let's face up to the fact that God can do anything He pleases. His actions are always righteous, and we don't have a leg to stand on if we think we can rightfully call Him unfair or unjust. Our responsibility is simply to believe what God has said.

SIX

The God of the Weather

For I know that the LORD is great, and that our Lord is above all gods. Whatsoever the LORD pleased, that did he in heaven, and in earth, in the seas, and all deep places. He causeth the vapours to ascend from the ends of the earth; he maketh lightnings for the rain; he bringeth the wind out of his treasuries (Psalm 135:5-7).

Behold, the name of the LORD cometh from far, burning with his anger, and the burden thereof is heavy: his lips are full of indignation, and his tongue as a devouring fire...And the LORD shall cause his glorious voice to be heard, and shall show the lighting down of his arm, with the indignation of his anger, and with the flame of a devouring fire, with scattering, and tempest, and hail-stones (Is. 30:27,30).

He sendeth forth his commandment upon earth: his word runneth very swiftly. He giveth snow like wool: he scattereth the hoarfrost like ashes. He casteth forth his ice

*like morsels: who can stand before his cold? He sendeth
out his word, and melteth them: he causeth his wind to
blow, and the waters flow* (Psalm 147:15-18).

*But the LORD is the true God, he is the living God, and an
everlasting king: at his wrath the earth shall tremble, and
the nations shall not be able to abide his indignation. Thus
shall ye say unto them, The gods that have not made the
heavens and the earth, even they shall perish from the
earth, and from under these heavens. He hath made the
earth by his power, he hath established the world by his
wisdom, and hath stretched out the heavens by his discre-
tion. When he uttereth his voice, there is a multitude of
waters in the heavens, and he causeth the vapours to
ascend from the ends of the earth; he maketh lightnings
with rain, and bringeth forth the wind out of his treasures*
(Jer. 10:10-13).

*For, lo, he that formeth the mountains, and createth the
wind, and declareth unto man what is his thought, that
maketh the morning darkness, and treadeth upon the high
places of the earth, The LORD, The God of hosts, is his
name* (Amos 4:13).

*And they feared exceedingly, and said one to another,
What manner of man is this, that even the wind and the
sea obey him?* (Mark 4:41).

Does God have control over the weather? Such a question
almost seems absurd, yet we are living in a day when
many Christians don't know who is in control of this earth.
Because of erroneous teaching, many suppose that God has
no rights to, or control over, this planet.[1] Some mistakenly

---

[1]For an in-depth study of this subject, I recommend *Modern Myths About Satan And
Spiritual Warfare* by David Kirkwood, Ethnos Press

claim that since Scripture says that Satan is the "god of this world" (2 Cor. 4:4), Satan must be the one who controls the weather. But such an assumption doesn't stand the scrutiny of Scripture.

Scores of Bible passages prove beyond any doubt that God is, as Jesus called Him, "Lord of heaven and earth" (Luke 10:21). The Greek word for *earth* is "ge," which refers to the physical planet. (From this word we get our word *geography*.) Although Satan is the god of this world, he is not god of the earth. He is god of the kosmos, or "world's system." Psalm 24:1 says that

> "the earth is the LORD'S, and the fulness thereof; the world, and they that dwell therein."

God is certainly sovereign over the elements, and as we shall see, He can use them to facilitate His wrath. In the Bible, God takes responsibility for floods, winds, earthquakes, fires, hurricanes, tornadoes, droughts, famines, pestilences, storms and more. Let's consider just a few examples of His control of the elements.

In Genesis 6:17, God said,

> "And, behold, I, even I, do bring a flood of waters upon the earth, to destroy all flesh, wherein is the breath of life, from under heaven; and every thing that is in the earth shall die."

This was a direct act of God, not something He only permitted.

In Genesis 8:1, "God made a wind to pass over the earth" at the end of the flood, and the waters subsided.

Genesis 19:24-25 states,

> "Then the LORD rained upon Sodom and upon
> Gomorrah brimstone and fire from the LORD out of
> heaven; And he overthrew those cities, and all the plain,
> and all the inhabitants of the cities, and that which grew
> upon the ground."

In Genesis 41 we read how God revealed future knowledge of the climate to Pharaoh. Verses 28-32 say,

> This is the thing which I have spoken unto Pharaoh:
> What God is about to do he showeth unto Pharaoh.
> Behold, there come seven years of great plenty through-
> out all the land of Egypt: And there shall arise after
> them seven years of famine; and all the plenty shall be
> forgotten in the land of Egypt; and the famine shall
> consume the land; And the plenty shall not be known in
> the land by reason of that famine following; for it shall
> be very grievous. And for that the dream was doubled
> unto Pharaoh twice; it is because the thing is estab-
> lished by God, and God will shortly bring it to pass.

The very fact that God revealed this to Pharaoh years in
advance reveals His complete control over rain and famine.

Years later the Egyptians endured God's judgment as their
nation suffered through ten plagues. God's sovereignty over
all of nature was revealed in those plagues, consummated
with the death of all the firstborn in Egypt.

In Exodus 10:13 we read that,

> "Moses stretched forth his rod over the land of Egypt,
> and the LORD brought an east wind upon the land all
> that day, and all that night; and when it was morning,

the east wind brought the locusts" that plagued Egypt. Verse 19 says, "And the LORD turned a mighty strong west wind, which took away the locusts, and cast them into the Red sea; there remained not one locust in all the coasts of Egypt."

We should never doubt that God controls the wind.

Exodus 14:21 says,

"And Moses stretched out his hand over the sea; and the LORD caused the sea to go back by a strong east wind all that night, and made the sea dry land, and the waters were divided."

In Numbers 11:31 we read that

"there went forth a wind from the LORD, and brought quails from the sea."

In 1 Samuel 7:10, God sent a great thunderstorm upon the Philistines, allowing Israel to defeat them in battle.

In 1 Samuel 12:16-18, God sent a terrible storm to show His displeasure over Israel's desiring a king to rule over them.

In 2 Samuel 21:1, King David sought God as to why Israel was suffering three years of famine, and God's reply was, "It is for Saul, and for his bloody house, because he slew the Gibeonites." How do you suppose God feels about our national stand on abortion, shedding innocent blood?

In 1 Kings 17:1, Elijah prophesied God's judgment upon Israel by means of a three-and-a-half-year drought.

In 2 Kings 8:1, Elisha warned a Shunammite woman that

God had called for a seven year famine in her land.

In 2 Chronicles 7:13, God said He would shut up heaven, send locusts to devour the land, and pestilence among His people.

Psalm 48:7 says of God,

> "Thou breakest the ships of Tarshish with an east wind."

In Psalms 148:7-8 ,we are told to praise God for fire, hail, snow, vapours and stormy winds that fulfill His Word.

In Isaiah 14:30, God said He would kill with a famine.

In Isaiah 28:2, God sent "tempest of hail, destroying storms, flood of mighty waters overflowing" as a form of judgment.

In Isaiah 29:6 we read,

> "Thou shalt be visited of the LORD of hosts with thunder, and with earthquake, and great noise, with storm and tempest [a violent windstorm, frequently accompanied by rain, snow, or hail] and the flame of devouring fire."

In Jeremiah 14:12-16, God promised severe judgment upon false prophets and their followers:

> "I will consume them by the sword, and by the famine, and by the pestilence."

In Jeremiah 16:3-4, God pronounced judgment on families, promising,

"They shall die of grievous deaths...they shall be consumed by the sword, and by famine; and their carcasses shall be meat for the fowls of heaven, and for the beasts of the earth."

In Jeremiah 24:10, God said,

"I will send the sword, the famine, and the pestilence, among them, till they be consumed from off the land that I gave unto them and to their fathers."

In Jeremiah 27:8; 34:17; 42:17; and 44:12-13, God repeatedly pronounced the judgment of sword, pestilence and famine upon those under His judgment.

Ezekiel 5:16 says,

"When I shall send upon them the evil arrows of famine, which shall be for their destruction, and which I will send to destroy you: and I will increase the famine upon you, and will break your staff of bread."

In Ezekiel 13:13, God sent wind storms, overflowing showers and hail.

In Ezekiel 38:22-23, God said He would plead against a wicked nation with pestilence, bloodshed, floods, hailstones and fire. Verse 23 says,

"Thus will I magnify myself, and sanctify myself; and I will be known in the eyes of many nations, and they shall know that I am the LORD."

Amos predicted seven times in the first two chapters of his book that God would "send a fire." Each one of those fires was to devour either cities or houses. Later in 4:6-13, God further stated that He would send a famine in the land, followed by droughts in some cities and floods in others. This would be followed by scorching weather and sickly vegetation, and then by an abundance of destructive pests and an epidemic of diseases.

Ask Jonah if God controls the weather! As he was running from his mission, God sent a "great wind into the sea, and there was a mighty tempest in the sea, so that the ship was like to be broken" (Jonah 1:4). After confessing his sin to those on the ship, we read that they "took up Jonah, and cast him forth into the sea; and the sea ceased from her raging. Then the men feared the LORD exceedingly, and offered a sacrifice unto the LORD, and made vows."

As we continue through Jonah's story, we read of God's sovereignty over not only the weather, but the plant and animal kingdoms as well. God prepared a "great fish" to swallow Jonah and to later vomit him out on the shore. He also prepared a large gourd to grow up overnight to protect Jonah from the hot sun, and then prepared a worm to eat it. Finally, God prepared a scorching east wind that beat upon Jonah's head. Jonah's book alone should be enough to convince anyone of God's sovereignty over everything.

In Nahum 1:1-8, God had His way in judgment by hurricanes, storms, droughts, quakes, fires and floods.

Revelation 18:8 says,

> "Therefore shall her plagues come in one day, death, and mourning, and famine; and she shall be utterly burned with fire: for strong is the Lord God who judgeth her."

According to Zechariah 14:17-19, those nations that refuse

to worship the Lord during the millennial reign of Christ will suffer famine.

> "And if the family of Egypt go not up, and come not, that have no rain; there shall be the plague, wherewith the LORD will smite the heathen that come not up to keep the feast of tabernacles. This shall be the punishment of Egypt, and the punishment of all nations that come not up to keep the feast of tabernacles."

These are just a few examples of the Lord's control of the elements and His powerful judgments being poured out in the form of severe weather and natural disasters. Insurance companies call these things "acts of God," while many modern preachers call them acts of Satan. Isn't it sad that secular insurance companies promote a more biblical theology concerning natural disasters than do many of God's preachers?

When the devastating January, 1994 earthquake shook Los Angeles, remarkably few lives were lost. Because the quake struck very early in the morning and on a national holiday, most schools and businesses were not open. Had it occurred three hours later on a regular day, no doubt thousands would have died. I heard newscasters remind us that day of "a merciful hand of Providence," and later, many stories were broadcasted of people's miraculous protection and survival. A few days later, I read an article in my local newspaper titled, "Earthquake Rocks Porn Industry":

> The overwhelming media coverage of last week's California earthquake failed to mention that the quake's epicenter is the hub of America's $3 billion X-rated video industry. The triangle formed by the San Fernando Valley communities of Chatsworth, Northridge and

Canoga Park—tightly encircling the epicenter of the powerful quake—contains nearly 70 companies that crank out more than 95 percent of the roughly 1,400 pornographic videos made every year in the United States. So far, this coincidence of cataclysm-and-Gomorrah appears to have gone unnoticed by California's feisty religious right, but no one who works in the entertainment industry's shadow side expects that situation to last. "Can you imagine how (the fundamentalists) are going to leap on this when the smoke clears?" said a director who works for several Northridge studios. "They're gonna have a field day of 'I told-you-sos' down in Orange County. They'll say it's God's retribution, His personal destruction of America's most wicked city." God's will or not, there is no doubt that the devastation in California's video-Sodom has been close to apocalyptic. A telephone survey of various Northridge and other Valley-area studios discloses that—with no exception—every company has suffered some major damage, much of it immobilizing (*Dayton Daily News*, 1/26/94 p. C4).

Unfortunately, the quoted concerns of that porn producer went unrealized. A Los Angeles pastor appeared on a national Christian television program and assured his audience that the earthquake was not God's judgment because God doesn't send earthquakes. He reasoned that God wouldn't cause an earthquake because people died and many "innocent" people suffered from its effects. But did his reasoning concur with the Bible?

Korah and his family believed that God sends killer quakes. In Numbers 16, Korah, his wife and their sons and daughters perished in an earthquake. God opened the earth and they all "went down alive into the pit, and the earth closed upon them: and they perished from among the congregation" (Num. 16:31-34)

Does God cause earthquakes? Consider the following verses:

> Then the earth shook and trembled; the foundations also of the hills moved and were shaken, because he [God] was wroth (Psalm 18:7).

> The voice of thy thunder was in the heaven: the lightnings lightened the world: the earth trembled and shook (Psalm 77:18).

> And they shall go into the holes of the rocks, and into the caves of the earth, for fear of the LORD, and for the glory of his majesty, when he ariseth to shake terribly the earth (Isaiah 2:19).

> The foundations of the earth do shake....The earth shall reel to and fro like a drunkard (Isaiah 24:18,20).

> For in my jealousy and in the fire of my wrath have I spoken, Surely in that day there shall be a great shaking in the land of Israel (Ezekiel 38:19).

> For thus saith the LORD of hosts; Yet once, it is a little while, and I will shake the heavens, and the earth, and the sea, and the dry land (Haggai 2:6).

> And great earthquakes shall be in divers places, and famines, and pestilences; and fearful sights and great signs shall there be from heaven (Luke 21:11).

There was an earthquake when the Law was given to

Moses according to Exodus 19:18.

There was an earthquake when Jesus died on the cross according to Matthew 27:54.

There was an earthquake when Jesus was raised from the dead according to Matthew 28:2.

Jesus stated in Matthew 24:7 that His imminent return would be marked by an increase of earthquakes in various places.

There was an earthquake when the believers were praying together in Acts 4:31.

There was an earthquake when Paul and Silas were jailed in Acts 16:26.

There are earthquakes mentioned in Revelation 6:12 and 8:5 when the sixth and seventh seals are opened.

There's an earthquake mentioned in Revelation 11:13. Seven-thousand people will perish in it.

There is an earthquake in Revelation 11:19 at the seventh trumpet judgment.

There is an earthquake in Revelation 16:18 at the pouring out of the seventh vial judgment.

In Frank Bartleman's eyewitness account of the great Azusa Street revival at the turn of the century, he shared the following words about the 1906 San Francisco earthquake:

> Sunday, April 15, the Lord called me to ten days of special prayer. I felt greatly burdened but had no idea of what He had particularly in mind. But He had a work

for me, and wanted to prepare me for it. Wednesday, April 18, the terrible San Francisco earthquake came, which also devastated the surrounding cities and county. No less than ten thousand lost their lives in San Francisco alone. I felt a deep conviction that the Lord was answering our prayers for a revival in His own way. "When Thy judgments are in the earth, the inhabitants of the world learn righteousness."—Isaiah 26:9. A tremendous burden of prayer came upon me that the people might not be indifferent to His voice....I found the earthquake had opened many hearts. I was distributing especially my last tract, "The Last Call." It seemed very appropriate after the earthquake. Sunday, April 22, I took 10,000 of these to the New Testament Church. The workers seized them eagerly and scattered them quickly throughout the city.

Nearly every pulpit in the land was working overtime to prove that God had nothing to do with earthquakes and thus allay the fears of the people. The Spirit was striving to knock at hearts with conviction, through this judgment. I felt indignation that the preachers should be used of Satan to drown out His voice....Even the teachers in the schools labored hard to convince the children that God was not in earthquakes. The devil put on a big propaganda on this line.

Bartleman goes on to tell about writing a tract about the earthquake after a night of intercession:

I seemed to feel the wrath of God against the people and to withstand it in prayer. He showed me He was terribly grieved at their obstinacy in the face of His judgment on sin. San Francisco was a terribly wicked city. He showed me all hell was being moved to drown out His voice in the earthquake, if possible. The message He had given me was to counteract this influence. Men had been denying His presence in the earthquake.[2]

When San Francisco suffered another terrible earthquake in 1989, this same story was repeated. Preachers were working overtime trying to convince Christians that God had nothing to do with it, claiming it was just an act of nature.

The New Agers were somewhat in agreement with those preachers, except they claimed that "Mother Nature" was upset with us earthlings for harming the ozone layer, the sea turtles, the rain forests and the dolphins. Actually, the New Agers were closer to the truth than many Christian preachers, because they were at least saying the earthquake was the result of some higher power's displeasure with humans! How sad that so many in our nation are more afraid of Mother Nature than Father God!

SEVEN

The Storms of Job, Jonah and Jesus

I form the light, and create darkness: I make peace, and create evil: I the LORD do all these things (Isaiah 45:7).

That ye may be the children of your Father which is in heaven: for he maketh his sun to rise on the evil and on the good, and sendeth rain on the just and on the unjust (Matt. 5:45).

Certainly you're convinced by now that not all negative things come from Satan. As we've repeatedly seen, God takes the credit for quite a few things we consider adverse. This is not to say, however, that Satan bears no responsibility for negative things in the world today. For example, Satan, not God, is the one who tempts people to sin, and thus he shares responsibility for all the sin in the world. But when we speak of severe weather, natural disasters and the like, we cannot escape the fact that God is in sovereign control. And when Satan is given rare credit in the Bible for such things, it's clear that he can only operate with God's permission.

To help our understanding of this crucial subject, let's consider a few biblical examples of severe weather, literal storms in the lives of Job, Jonah and Jesus. We'll begin with Job.

In the first chapter of Job, we read of Satan, who had access to the throne of God, presenting himself there. God mentioned His servant Job, praising him for his fear of God and hatred of sin. Satan, however, accused Job of serving God only because of the blessings he received. Let the blessings stop, accused Satan, and Job would curse God to His face.

God took Satan at his challenge, and allowed the "hedge" around Job to be removed. Satan was given permission to attack, and consequently, Job's sons and daughters were killed in a violent wind storm. Next, the so-called "fire of God" fell on Job's sheep and servants, killing them all. Finally, other servants were killed by an attacking army, and the other flocks and herds were stolen or killed as well. Only one individual escaped each tragedy to deliver the bad news to Job.

Job's reaction to his tragedies was remarkable:

> Then Job arose, and rent his mantle, and shaved his head, and fell down upon the ground, and worshipped, And said, Naked came I out of my mother's womb, and naked shall I return thither: the LORD gave, and the LORD hath taken away; blessed be the name of the LORD. In all this Job sinned not, nor charged God foolishly (Job 1:20-22).

Take note that the Bible declared that Job *did not charge God foolishly, even though he blamed God for taking away all that he had.* We know, unlike Job, that God did not actually kill Job's children, servants and livestock. But Job knew, unlike so many modern Christians, that God is sovereign. God was in control and allowed Job's trials, and they couldn't have happened otherwise. God never rebuked Job for saying, "The Lord gave, and the Lord hath taken away."

> Then said his [Job's] wife unto him, Dost thou still retain thine integrity? curse God, and die. But he said unto her, Thou speakest as one of the foolish women speaketh. What? shall we receive good at the hand of God, and shall we not receive evil? *In all this did not Job sin with his lips* (Job 2:9-10, emphasis added).

Again, notice that Job said that God had sent evil, but the Bible declared he did not sin with his lips. Job understood God's sovereignty. Such a tragedy could never have occurred apart from God's will or permission.

My main point is that Satan obviously does have the ability to cause violent storms. He is under God's sovereign control. Satan couldn't harm Job without God's permission. In fact, during Job's first trial, Satan was forbidden by God to touch Job's body, and he didn't. God has a collar and leash on the devil.

Jonah also faced a great storm as he was fleeing from the presence of the Lord on a ship in the Mediterranean Sea. Who was given the credit for that storm?

> But the LORD sent out a great wind into the sea, and there was a mighty tempest in the sea, so that the ship was like to be broken (Jonah 1:4).

It was not Satan, but the Lord who caused the great wind that threatened the lives of those on the ship. By casting lots, the crew determined that Jonah was the one responsible for their calamity. He then confessed his sin and told them what to do:

> And he said unto them, Take me up, and cast me forth into the sea; so shall the sea be calm unto you: for I know that for my sake this great tempest is upon you. Nevertheless the men rowed hard to bring it to the land; but they could not: for the sea wrought, and was tempestuous against them. Wherefore they cried unto the LORD, and said, We beseech thee, O LORD, we beseech thee, let us not perish for this man's life, and lay not upon us innocent blood: for thou, O LORD, hast done as it pleased thee. So they took up Jonah, and cast him forth into the sea: and the sea ceased from her raging. Then the men feared the LORD exceedingly, and offered a sacrifice unto the LORD, and made vows (Jonah 1:12-16).

Clearly this incident was a direct act of God. The result was that it caused such fear of God to fall on that ship's pagan crew that they "offered a sacrifice unto the LORD, and made vows" (Jonah 1:16).

As the story unfolds, we read that God prepared a great fish to deliver Jonah back to dry land. Later, God prepared a huge gourd, sent a worm to eat that gourd, and then added a hot east wind to teach Jonah a lesson about His mercy. God's sovereign hand extended over the storm, the casting of lots, the marine, plant and insect life, and the scorching winds. He's sovereign.

One final storm we need to consider is one that Jesus faced as He crossed the Sea of Galilee:

> And there arose a great storm of wind, and the waves

beat into the ship, so that it was now full. And he was in the hinder part of the ship, asleep on a pillow: and they awake him, and say unto him, Master, carest thou not that we perish? And he arose, and rebuked the wind, and said unto the sea, Peace, be still. And the wind ceased, and there was a great calm. And he said unto them, Why are ye so fearful? how is it that ye have no faith? And they feared exceedingly, and said one to another, What manner of man is this, that even the wind and the sea obey him? (Mark 4:37-41).

Many say that Satan was responsible for that storm, but Scripture doesn't say so. Neither does it say that God sent it. Yet we can be sure, without a doubt, that storm didn't catch God by surprise. He knew it was coming (He knows everything), and He led His Son to cross the Sea of Galilee when He knew it was coming. We can also be sure that it was under God's sovereign control. He could have stopped it at any time.

All that being true, why would God ever lead His divine Son into a situation that was potentially life-threatening? (Obviously, it was not God's will for Jesus to die that day on the Sea of Galilee. He was destined to die upon the cross.)

There are many possible answers to that question which are beyond the scope of our study. One possibility I will briefly mention is that Jesus had to be tempted in all ways like us in order to prove Himself sinless and thus qualify to be our Savior (see Heb. 4:15). In this incident, Jesus would have been tempted to doubt God and be fearful, but He wasn't, and passed the test.

Some will claim that it *must* have been Satan who sent the storm that day on Galilee, because God would never cause something that might have harmed His Son. But we've already learned that Satan can do nothing without God's permission. If Satan sent the storm that day on Galilee, he could have only done it with God's allowance, and that being the case, then God obviously allowed Satan to do something that could have potentially harmed God's Son. So the same question with a slight variation could be posed: Why would God allow something to happen (and He did) that might have harmed His Son? Moreover, we know that it wasn't God's intention for Jesus to be harmed in any way by that storm. It was God's intention for Jesus to calm the storm.

Some say that it must have been Satan who sent the storm because Jesus *rebuked* it. Surely He wouldn't rebuke something God caused. But, again, that logic is not convincing. God can cause storms and God can stop them by rebuking them. We read in Psalm 107: "For He [God] commandeth, and raiseth the stormy wind, which lifteth up the waves thereof....He maketh the storm a calm, so that the waves thereof are still" (Ps. 107:25,29).

Jesus didn't rebuke God the Father—He rebuked the wind and waves. (Neither did He rebuke the devil.)

Some try to remove the responsibility for severe weather from God by blaming it on Adam's sin and how that affected all of nature. It is certainly true that the whole creation suffers from the fall of Adam (see Romans 8:17-25). But remember that God is the one who cursed the ground, and He is the one who subjected the creation to futility (see Romans 8:20). Even if hurricanes are random acts of fallen nature, God is at least partly responsible (and how could we ever believe in anything being truly "random," knowing our omniscient and omnipotent God?)

Paul was once caught in a terrible typhoon while en route by ship to Rome (see Acts 27:14-44). We read that an angel appeared to him and assured him that all would be well, yet the storm continued! The Lord could have stopped the storm that very moment, but He didn't. And notice that Paul didn't attempt to rebuke the storm, but simply trusted that God knew what He was doing. Ultimately, the ship ran aground on the island of Malta, where God used Paul to start a revival. Truly, God causes all things to work together for good to them that love God, to them who are the called according to His purpose (Rom. 8:28).

There are, of course, other negative things in our world besides severe weather. To bring balance to this whole subject, let me say that we can't blame every trouble we face on Satan or God. The majority of the trouble in the world is caused by people's sins and carelessness. When someone consumes alcohol and develops cirrhosis of the liver, or when a person drives recklessly and suffers an accident, neither God nor Satan can be blamed. Sickness can be the result of poor eating habits. Relationships can be ruined by selfishness. Much more could be said about this subject, but it is not my purpose to explain all suffering in the world. I only want you to understand what God clearly claims responsibility for in His Word.

EIGHT

🛡

Is America Experiencing the
Judgment of God?

*The wicked shall be turned into hell, and all the nations
that forget God* (Psalm 9:17).

*Righteousness exalteth a nation: but sin is a reproach to
any people* (Prov. 14:34).

*"If I shut up heaven that there be no rain, or if I command
the locusts to devour the land, or if I send pestilence
among my people; If my people, which are called by my
name, shall humble themselves, and pray, and seek my
face, and turn from their wicked ways; then will I hear
from heaven, and will forgive their sin, and will heal their
land"* (2 Chron. 7:13-14).

Please note the final above-quoted scripture, the second
half of which is so often quoted in reference to what we
must do to bring revival to our nation. Yet the first half, which
is rarely quoted, tells us *why* we should humble ourselves,
seek God's face, pray and turn from our wicked ways. It tells

us that God sends drought, devouring insects and epidemic diseases upon deserving nations, and when those judgments begin falling upon a nation, it's a sure sign of God's disapproval and the need for repentance. Isaiah 26:9 says,

> "When thy judgments are in the earth, the inhabitants of the world will learn righteousness."

Certainly the United States of America is experiencing the judgment of God, and we deserve it, for we've turned our backs on a gracious God. Is it not true, as Jesus told us, that to whom much is given, much is required? Unlike many other countries, the United States was founded as a Christian one, and consequently, God has blessed us immeasurably. We have, however, forsaken Him, and His wrath is increasingly upon us. Yet we live in such a spiritually cold day that most don't (or perhaps won't) recognize the obvious. Few will admit that America is under God's strong hand of judgment!

Many great leaders in the past recognized the wrath of God when it fell upon our nation. In 1781, Thomas Jefferson said in his *Notes on the State of Virginia* (part of which are engraved on the Jefferson Memorial in Washington, D.C.):

> God who gave us life gave us liberty. And can the liberties of a nation be thought secure when we have removed their only firm basis, a conviction in the minds of the people that these liberties are of the gift of God? That they are not to be violated but with His wrath? Indeed, I tremble for my country when I reflect that God is just; that His justice cannot sleep forever.[1]

In 1863, President Abraham Lincoln issued a historic proclamation of National Day of Fasting:

Whereas, the Senate of the United States devoutly

---

[1]*America's God and Country Encyclopedia of Quotations*, p. 323

recognizing the Supreme Authority and just government of Almighty God in all the affairs of men and of nations, has, by a resolution, requested the President to designate and set apart a day for national prayer and humiliation:

And whereas, it is the duty of nations as well as of men to owe their dependence upon the overruling power of God, to confess their sins and transgressions in humble sorrow yet with assured hope that genuine repentance will lead to mercy and pardon, and to recognize the sublime truth, announced in the Holy Scriptures and proven by all history: that those nations only are blessed whose God is the Lord:

And, insomuch as we know that by His divine law, nations like individuals are subjected to punishments and chastisement in this world, may we not justly fear that the awful calamity of civil war, which now desolates the land may be but a punishment inflicted upon us for our presumptuous sins to the needful end of our national reformation as a whole people? We have been the recipients of the choicest bounties of Heaven. We have been preserved these many years in peace and prosperity. We have grown in numbers, wealth and power as no other nation has ever grown. But we have forgotten God. We have forgotten the gracious Hand which preserved us in peace, and multiplied and enriched and strengthened us; and we have vainly imagined, in the deceitfulness of our hearts, that all these blessings were produced by some superior wisdom and virtue of our own. Intoxicated with unbroken success, we have become too self-sufficient to feel the necessity of redeeming and preserving grace, too proud to pray to the God that made us! It behooves us then to humble ourselves before the offended Power, to confess our national sins and to pray for clemency and forgiveness.[2]

God is once again visiting our nation with judgment. Read carefully a sampling of the prophets of old, and see if they have a familiar ring to them:

> Thou shalt be visited of the LORD of hosts with thunder, and with earthquake, and great noise, with storm and tempest, and the flame of devouring fire (Is. 29:6).

> God is jealous, and the LORD revengeth; the LORD revengeth, and is furious; the LORD will take vengeance on his adversaries, and he reserveth wrath for his enemies. The LORD is slow to anger, and great in power, and will not at all acquit the wicked: the LORD hath his way in the whirlwind and in the storm, and the clouds are the dust of his feet. He rebuketh the sea, and maketh it dry, and drieth up all the rivers: Bashan languisheth, and Carmel, and the flower of Lebanon languisheth. The mountains quake at him, and the hills melt, and the earth is burned at his presence, yea, the world, and all that dwell therein. Who can stand before his indignation? and who can abide in the fierceness of his anger? his fury is poured out like fire, and the rocks are thrown down by him. The LORD is good, a strong hold in the day of trouble; and he knoweth them that trust in him. But with an overrunning flood he will make an utter end of the place thereof, and darkness shall pursue his enemies (Nahum 1:2-8).

In the preceding passage of Scripture Nahum spoke of God "having His way" by whirlwinds (tornados), storms,

---

[2]*America's God and Country Encyclopedia of Quotations*, pp. 383-384

droughts, quakes, fires and floods. We have often prayed for God to show up and have "His way" in our nation, and now He has!

Below is a list of the most costly catastrophes in the history of the United States of America. Note that they've all occurred since 1989. I have included the month, year, disaster and insured loss.[3]

> Aug. 1992, Hurricane Andrew (Florida), $15.5 Billion
> July 1993, Midwest Floods, $10 Billion
> Jan. 1994, Los Angeles Earthquake, $7 Billion
> Oct. 1989, Loma Prieta Earthquake, $6 Billion
> Sept. 1989, Hurricane Hugo (South Carolina),
> $4.2 Billion
> Jan. 1995, California Floods, $2 Billion
> Oct. 1995, Hurricane Opal (Florida), $2 Billion[4]
> Oct. 1991, Oakland Fire, $1.7 Billion
> Mar. 1993, 24-state winter storm, $1.6 Billion
> Sept. 1992, Hurricane Iniki, $1.6 Billion
> Mar. 1995, California Floods, $1.3 Billion
> Dec. 1993 Wind/Freeze (41 States), $880 Million
> Apr. 1992 Wind, Hail, Tornadoes (Texas and OK),
> $760 Million

So many American Christians don't believe God would do anything to harm the United States because we are (supposedly) His only witness in the world (which is no longer true). That was exactly how Israel felt when they heard of God's judgment coming upon them. "God won't do that to us because He loves us" they reasoned. All we need to do is open our Bibles and read what God did to Israel, His chosen people. Though God has blessed us and made us great, He's now judging us, like He did Israel, for our backslidden ways.

---

[3]Insurance Information Institute and USA Today, 3/14/95
[4]*Time Magazine*, October 16, 1995

George Mason, called the "Father of the Bill of Rights," stated his views on our national accountability before God during the debates of the Constitutional Convention:

> As nations cannot be rewarded or punished in the next world, they must be in this. By an inevitable chain of causes and effects, Providence punishes national sins, by national calamities.[5]

In Leviticus 26:14-39, God said that if the nation of Israel refused to obey His Word, He would send a total of eighty-one different curses which included terrorism, war, destruction of cities, loss of crops, national destruction, bad weather, blight upon fruit trees, epidemic diseases in crowded cities, suicide, low wages for work and more. Think about it for a moment. Do any of these things sound like America's problems?

In Deuteronomy 28:15-68, God listed 112 curses that would befall the nation of Israel for forsaking the Lord. Included in that list were curses upon their children, crops, herds, flocks and financial institutions. They would suffer sickness, crop failure, war, captivity, business failure, poverty, persecution, insanity, slavery, cannibalism, extreme poverty and death. Once again, don't those have a familiar sound to them in our nation? As William Newell comments,

> The God of the twentieth century is not the God of the Bible, but the God of the vain imaginations of shallow men,—men who will not look honestly at history (as in the Flood, or Sodom and Gomorrah); nay, who will not look honestly at present events! Preachers are found by the thousands who pooh-pooh the thought that the great calamities, such as the late war, and that now are looming, are judgments of God; that great droughts or

---

[5]*America's God and Country Encyclopedia of Quotations*, p. 423

floods or storms are sent by Him. Like the hardened wretches whom Ezekiel saw, they say, "Jehovah seeth us not; Jehovah hath forsaken the land."[6]

Today, more than ever, we need men and women who will cry out like Jeremiah did:

> O LORD, are not thine eyes upon the truth? thou hast stricken them, but they have not grieved; thou hast consumed them, but they have refused to receive correction: they have made their faces harder than a rock; they have refused to return. Therefore I said, Surely these are poor; they are foolish: for they know not the way of the LORD, nor the judgment of their God (Jer. 5:3-4).

Today, where are those who have come off their knees with a powerful word from heaven? Our modern prophets have become mere echoes instead of voices, mimicking whatever is popular! Instead of declaring the message of the wrath of God, they speak of peace and prosperity.

Our nation is without the fear of God and is hanging by a thread. Without thought of the consequences, we continue to promote perversion from Hollywood to Nashville, massacre millions of unborn children and follow after what feels good. Deploring God and His righteous ways, our nation increasingly emulates Sodom and Gomorrah. God is calling this nation to repent or experience His wrath to an even greater degree!

We must quickly turn from our sins and come humbly back to God. If our pulpits won't preach the truth, God will still get His message across. He knows how to get our attention!

---

[6]*Romans, Verse by Verse*, William R. Newell, p. 46

NINE

What Then Shall We Do?

It may be that the house of Judah will hear all the evil which I purpose to do unto them; that they may return every man from his evil way; that I may forgive their iniquity and their sin....It may be they will present their supplication before the LORD, and will return every one from his evil way: for great is the anger and the fury that the LORD hath pronounced against this people
(Jer. 36:3,7).

Who is a God like unto thee, that pardoneth iniquity, and passeth by the transgression of the remnant of his heritage? he retaineth not his anger for ever, because he delighteth in mercy. He will turn again, he will have compassion upon us; he will subdue our iniquities; and thou wilt cast all their sins into the depths of the sea
(Micah 7:18-19).

O LORD, I have heard thy speech, and was afraid: O LORD, revive thy work in the midst of the years, in the

midst of the years make known; in wrath remember mercy
(Hab. 3:2).

*I know, O LORD, that thy judgments are right, and that
thou in faithfulness hast afflicted me. Let, I pray thee, thy
merciful kindness be for my comfort, according to thy
word unto thy servant. Let thy tender mercies come unto
me, that I may live: for thy law is my delight....My flesh
trembleth for fear of thee; and I am afraid of thy judgments* (Psalm 119:75-77,120).

*When thy judgments are in the earth, the inhabitants of the
world will learn righteousness* (Is. 26:9).

I trust this book has spoken to you about the sad state of our
spiritually-sick nation and the pending judgments that
await us if we don't turn back to God. We desperately need
a heaven-sent revival in our land! But this revival will not
come until we turn our hearts by humbling ourselves, praying, seeking God's face and turning from our sins. We
certainly deserve all that has come upon us, but God is willing
to forgive, cleanse and heal us if we turn from our wickedness
and call on His mercy and grace.

> Before the decree bring forth, before the day pass as the
> chaff, before the fierce anger of the LORD come upon
> you, before the day of the LORD'S anger come upon
> you. Seek ye the LORD, all ye meek of the earth, which
> have wrought his judgment; seek righteousness, seek
> meekness: it may be ye shall be hid in the day of the
> LORD'S anger (Zeph. 2:2-3).

If we, as the people of God, will turn from our pride and
sin, I believe we will have a great opportunity to see another
national revival. Unless we see a sweeping revival of repen-

tance and humility, there is no hope for our nation.

Not long ago I was reading the book of Daniel and saw something I had never noticed before. As Daniel was studying the writings of the prophets, he noticed in particular the prophecies of Jeremiah. There he read of God's promise to restore the nation of Israel after a certain number of years of captivity to a foreign power. As Daniel figured out the time frame, he realized the time was near for Israel to be delivered from Babylon. This revelation caused him to be burdened with a spirit of intercession. He began to pour out his heart to God with strong words of repentance and supplication. He prayed and confessed sins, asking God for forgiveness and restoration.

His prayer in Daniel 9:3-19 almost seemed to jump off the pages as I read it. Unlike so many prayers we hear or pray today, Daniel's prayer had great substance to it. He was no novice when it came to seeking God, and his prayer reflected maturity and wisdom.

As I read Daniel's prayer for his nation, my heart was stirred. There was no haughtiness or arrogance in his appeal to God. He didn't command God (as some think they can do today), nor did he rebuke Satan. He simply and humbly implored God.

If Daniel were alive today and living in our nation, I believe he would pray in a very similar way. And with this in mind, I rewrote Daniel's prayer as if he were praying for America, for our leaders and churches.

I'm taking this prayer everywhere I travel and minister, challenging Christians across our great nation to pray it daily. I call it the *National Revival Prayer*:

We turn toward the Lord our God, to plead with Him in prayer and petition, with fasting and humility.
O Lord, great and awesome God, keeping Your covenant and mercy to those that love You, and to those that keep Your commandments; We have sinned! We have committed terrible sins! We have done very wickedly! We have rebelled by departing from Your commands and from Your laws written in Your Word. We have not obeyed the prophets, who spoke in Your Name to our presidents, our national leaders, to our parents, and to all the people of our nation.

O Lord, You are righteous, but today we are embarrassed and ashamed; every one of us, from the least to the greatest, because of the many ways we have sinned against You. O Lord, to each of us belongs embarrassment and shame, to our presidents, to our national leaders, and even to our parents, because we have sinned against You. Lord God, You are merciful and forgiving, even though we have rebelled against You. We have not obeyed Your Word, to follow Your laws which You gave us.

Yes, all of America has broken and violated Your law by disobeying Your Holy Word. And because we have refused to obey Your voice; the curse is poured upon us, the sworn judgments that are written in Your Word. And because we have sinned against You, You have fulfilled the words spoken against us, and against our leaders, by bringing upon us these great disasters. Just as it is written in the law of Moses, all these disasters and troubles have come upon us and yet we still have not turned our hearts toward You, by turning from our sins and paying attention to Your Word. You did not

94

hesitate to bring these disasters and troubles upon us, and You are righteous and just in everything You do, because we have not obeyed Your voice.

And now, O Lord our God, Who brought this great nation into existence with a mighty hand, and who has made Yourself known to this very day; We confess, we have sinned, we have committed much wickedness. O Lord, according to all Your righteousness, we beg You, let Your anger and Your wrath be turned away from our cities. We also realize and admit that because of our sins, and the sins of our parents, America and her people have become a reproach to the whole world.

Now also, O our God, hear the prayer and the petition of Your servants...please shine Your face upon the church that has become so barren! Do this for Your own glory! God, please listen and hear us, please look and see the hopelessness and despair among the people who are called by Your name.

We do not present these requests before You because we are righteous, but because we know You are great in mercy! O Lord, hear us and forgive us! O Lord, listen and do something quick! Don't delay! Do this for Your own glory, Lord, because this nation and Your people are called by Your name! In Jesus' Name, Amen!

TEN

The Only Way to Escape God's Eternal Wrath

For God has not appointed us to wrath, but to obtain salvation by our Lord Jesus Christ, (1 Thessalonians 5:9)

He that believeth on the Son hath everlasting life: and he that believeth not the Son shall not see life; but the wrath of God abideth on him (John 3:36).

The wrath of God that our nation is presently experiencing is but a foreshadowing of a much greater wrath that Americans will face if they don't turn from their wicked ways. That wrath is God's *eternal* wrath, because the Bible teaches that those who don't repent and believe the gospel will spend an eternity suffering in hell for their sins. Whether America as a whole ever repents and escapes God's temporal wrath, every individual must repent if he or she hopes to escape God's eternal wrath. In this chapter, I want to share with you exactly what you must do to escape that wrath.

One of the verses I quoted at the beginning of this chapter

promises us that if we'll believe, we'll receive life, but if we'll refuse to believe, God's wrath will abide upon us. God gives us all a choice: to believe or not to believe. Being made right with God is an act of trusting God and His Word. When we do, salvation becomes a reality in our lives.

Let's look at some clear facts from God's Word about this offer of salvation.

FACT #1: *Every Person Has Sinned Against God*

> As it is written, There is none righteous, no, not one (Rom. 3:10).

> For all have sinned, and come short of the glory of God (Rom. 3:23).

> If we say that we have no sin, we deceive ourselves, and the truth is not in us....If we say that we have not sinned, we make Him a liar, and His word is not in us (1 John 1:8,10)

No person can honestly say he is without sin. Everyone has broken God's laws. We have all willingly turned against what is right and have committed what is wrong. If you admit this then you're ready for the second fact.

FACT #2: *There Is An Eternal Cost For Your Sin*

> For the wrath of God is revealed from heaven against all ungodliness and unrighteousness of men (Rom. 1:18).

> There is a way which seemeth right unto a man, but the end thereof are the ways of death (Prov. 14:12).

> For the wages of sin is death; but the gift of God is eternal life through Jesus Christ our Lord (Rom. 6:23).

God's wrath against sin is revealed by death. In the Bible, *death* means "separation," and it's revealed in three forms: physical death, "the second death," and spiritual death. Sinning results in all three.

Physical death takes place when the spirit is separated from the body (see James 2:26). The second death is the judgment of final and eternal separation from God, when the unsaved are cast into the lake of fire (see Revelation 20:14). And spiritual death means being separated from God as a result of our sins (see Isaiah 59:2).

Because we're trapped in sin and separated from God, the third fact is obvious:

FACT #3: *You Cannot Save Yourself*

Jesus answered and said unto him, Verily, verily, I say unto thee, Except a man be born again, he cannot see the kingdom of God (John 3:3).

Not by works of righteousness which we have done, but according to his mercy he saved us (Titus 3:5).

For by grace are ye saved through faith; and that not of yourselves: it is the gift of God: Not of works, lest any man should boast (Eph. 2:8-9).

Therefore by the deeds of the law there shall no flesh be justified in his sight: for by the law is the knowledge of sin (Rom. 3:20).

We're all guilty of sin and have no way of clearing ourselves from God's condemnation. If we attempt to make ourselves better, we end up proving we can't. Our conscience keeps reminding us of our guilt, because we keep breaking

God's righteous laws. Our situation seems hopeless, except for the fact that:

FACT #4: *God's Love And Mercy Has Made A Way!*

> Jesus saith unto him, I am the way, the truth, and the life: no man cometh unto the Father, but by me (John 14:6).

> But God commendeth his love toward us, in that, while we were yet sinners, Christ died for us. Much more then, being now justified by his blood, we shall be saved from wrath through him (Rom. 5:8-9).

In His grace, God has sent Jesus to pay the penalty for our sins. He died for us, bearing the guilt for our sins. What a great proof of His love toward sinners! While we continued in our rebellion, Jesus paid the penalty for the sins of all humanity! How should we respond to His love?

FACT #5: *You Must Repent, Turning From Your Sins and Sinful Lifestyle*

> I tell you, Nay: but, except ye repent, ye shall all likewise perish (Luke 13:3).

> Repent ye therefore, and be converted, that your sins may be blotted out (Acts 3:19).

> Repent therefore of this thy wickedness, and pray God, if perhaps the thought of thine heart may be forgiven thee (Acts 8:22).

> Let the wicked forsake his way, and the unrighteous man his thoughts: and let him return unto the LORD, and he will have mercy upon him; and to our God, for he will abundantly pardon (Isaiah 55:7).

Repentance not only means being sorry for your sins; it means changing your mind about sin. True repentance means turning away from sin and turning to God and His ways.

FACT #6: *You Must Confess Your Sins To God, Calling Upon the Name Of The Lord in Sincere And Earnest Prayer*

If we confess our sins, he is faithful and just to forgive us our sins, and to cleanse us from all unrighteousness (1 John 1:9).

He that covereth his sins shall not prosper: but whoso confesseth and forsaketh them shall have mercy (Prov. 28:13).

And it shall come to pass, that whosoever shall call on the name of the Lord shall be saved (Acts 2:21).

Seek ye the LORD while he may be found, call ye upon him while he is near (Isaiah 55:6).

By calling on the Lord for forgiveness and mercy, you are admitting you've sinned, that you're unable to clear yourself from God's judgment, and that you're willing to forsake your sinful lifestyle and become obedient to God.

FACT #7: *You Must Personally Put Your Faith in Jesus Christ and Receive Him as Your Lord and Savior*

But as many as received him, to them gave he power to become the sons of God, even to them that believe on his name (John 1:12).

Jesus said unto him, If thou canst believe, all things are possible to him that believeth (Mark 9:23).

But without faith it is impossible to please him: for he

that cometh to God must believe that he is, and that he is a rewarder of them that diligently seek him (Hebrews 11:6).

And they said, Believe on the Lord Jesus Christ, and thou shalt be saved, and thy house (Acts 16:31).

Therefore I say unto you, What things soever ye desire, when ye pray, believe that ye receive them, and ye shall have them (Mark 11:24).

That if thou shalt confess with thy mouth the Lord Jesus, and shalt believe in thine heart that God hath raised him from the dead, thou shalt be saved. For with the heart man believeth unto righteousness; and with the mouth confession is made unto salvation (Rom. 10:9-10).

You must believe in your heart that Christ's death on the cross paid for all your sins. You must willingly and openly confess with your mouth that Jesus is Lord, the Risen Savior.

Right now, confess with your mouth what you believe in your heart about Christ and trust Him for your salvation! If you don't know what to say, pray something like this:

Dear God, I come to You as a sinner, confessing the fact that I have willingly sinned against You. I know I deserve judgment for my sins, but I believe that You sent Your only begotten Son, the Lord Jesus Christ into the world, and that He died on the cross to pay the debt for my sins. I ask You, right now, to forgive me and to come into my life as Lord and Savior. I turn my back on sin and trust You to forgive and cleanse me from every single sin I've committed. I renounce Satan's power in my mind and in my life. From this day on, I will live for Him who died for me. Thank You, Lord, for forgiving me! Help me live for You. This I pray and give You thanks, in Jesus' Name, Amen.

For the scripture saith, Whosoever believeth on him shall not be ashamed. For there is no difference between the Jew and the Greek: for the same Lord over all is rich unto all that call upon him. For whosoever shall call upon the name of the Lord shall be saved (Rom. 10:11-13).

If you've sincerely turned your life over to the Lordship of Jesus Christ, you'll desire to be as much like Jesus as possible. This can and will be accomplished through the power of God's Spirit working in you. Ask God to fill you with His Spirit. Walk in obedience to God's Word, the Bible. Read it every day. Spend quality time talking to God in prayer about every aspect of your life. Attend a church that teaches the Bible. Be baptized in water, making a public confession of your faith in Christ. Share your new life in Christ with others daily so they, too, will know the Truth!

If you need help or direction in any of these areas, please write me and I'll be happy to help. God bless you!

John Muncy
P.O. Box 377
Miamisburg, Ohio
45343-0377

BIBLIOGRAPHY

Bartleman, Frank, *Azusa Street,* Logos International, 1980

Boice, James Montgomery, *Romans*, Baker Book House, 1991

Federer, William J., *America's God and Country,* FAME Publishing, Inc., 1994

Hutson, Curtis, *Great Preaching On Hell,* Sword Of The Lord Publishers, 1989

Kirkwood, David, *God's Tests,* Ethnos Press, 1993

MacArthur, Jr., John, *Romans,* Moody Press, 1991

Newell, William R., *Romans Verse By Verse,* Kregel, 1994

Packer, J. I., *Knowing God,* Inter Varsity Press, 1973

Pink, Arthur W., *The Attributes of God,* Baker Book House, 1975

Torrey, R. A., *What The Bible Teaches,* Fleming H. Revell, 1900

Van Impe, Jack, *Sin's Explosion,* Jack Van Impe Ministries, 1988